THE
2003 ANNUAL:
Volume 2
Consulting

(The Forty-First Annual)

JOSSEY-BASS/PFEIFFER
A Wiley Imprint
www.pfeiffer.com

THE
2003 ANNUAL:
Volume 2
Consulting

(The Forty-First Annual)

Edited by Elaine Biech

JOSSEY-BASS/PFEIFFER
A Wiley Imprint
www.pfeiffer.com

Published by Jossey-Bass/Pfeiffer
A Wiley Imprint
989 Market Street, San Francisco, CA94103-1741   www.pfeiffer.com

Looseleaf ISBN:0-7879-6260-0
Paperback ISBN 0-7879-6265-1
ISSN 1046-333X

Jossey-Bass/Pfeiffer books and products are available through most bookstores. To contact Jossey-Bass/Pfeiffer directly call our Customer Care Department within the U.S. at 800-274-4434, outside the U.S. at 317-572-3985 or fax 317-572-4002.

Jossey-Bass/Pfeiffer also publishes its books in a variety of electronic formats. Some content that appears in print may not be available in electronic books.

Printed in the United States of America

Acquiring Editor: Martin Delahoussaye
Director of Development: Kathleen Dolan Davies
Developmental Editors: Susan Rachmeler and Rebecca Taff
Senior Production Editor: Dawn Kilgore
Manufacturing Supervisor: Becky Carreño

Printing   10   9   8   7   6   5   4   3   2   1

PREFACE

The *2003 Annual: Volume 2, Consulting,* is the forty-first volume in the *Annual* series, a collection of practical materials written for trainers, consultants, and performance-improvement technologists. This source for experiential learning activities, resource for instruments, and reference for cutting-edge articles has inspired human resource development (HRD) professionals for thirty-two years.

The *Annuals* are published as a set of two: Volume 1, Training, and Volume 2, Consulting. Materials in the training volume focus on skill building and knowledge enhancement. The training volume also features articles that enhance the skills and professional development of trainers. Materials in the consulting volume focus on intervention techniques and organizational systems. The consulting volume also features articles that enhance the skills and professional development of consultants.

Whether you are a trainer, a consultant, a facilitator, or a bit of each, you will find tools and techniques between the *Annual* covers. Trainers, are you looking for ideas to train a new department? Design a new training program? Refresh training that is a mainstay in your organization? Incorporate e-learning into your programs? Check out Volume 1. Consultants, are you searching for just the right team-building intervention? New concepts for coaching executives? Resources to send to your clients? A new approach to address communication? You will find it in Volume 2. Facilitators, are you seeking evaluation tools for teams? Feedback tools? Experiential activities to enhance learning? You will find answers in both volumes.

Both volumes provide you with the basics, such as conflict management and communication skills. Both volumes challenge you to use new techniques and models, such as storytelling and HR partnerships. Both volumes show you how to utilize technology throughout your efforts, such as evaluating e-learning and online communication. And both volumes introduce cutting-edge topics, such as measuring online learning readiness and retaining high-performance employees.

As you might expect, there is some overlap between the two volumes. Therefore, it is sometimes difficult for an editor to determine which volume is the best location for a submission. And, indeed, often submissions could be placed in either. As you search for resources, examine both volumes to find materials that will best meet your needs. You will find that, with a slight modification, you will be able to use activities, articles, and instruments from both volumes.

To ensure that you get the most from both the *Annuals,* be sure that you have a *Reference Guide* to help you identify all the materials available to you. The *Reference Guide* is a giant index to all the *Annuals* and the *Handbook of Structured Experiences,* Volumes I through X, that helps you locate just what you need based on topics and key words. A print version of the *Reference Guide* is available for volumes through 1999. An online supplement covering the years through 2003 can be found at www.pfeiffer.com/go/supplement.

There are good reasons that the *Annual* series has been around for over thirty years. In addition to the wide variety of topics and implementation levels, the *Annuals* provide materials that are applicable to varying circumstances. You will find instruments for individuals, teams, and organizations; experiential learning activities to round out workshops, team building, or consulting assignments; and articles to assign as pre-reading, to read to increase your knowledge base, or to use as reference materials in your writing tasks.

Probably the most important reason the *Annuals* are a success is that they are immediately ready to use. All of the materials in the *Annuals* may be duplicated for educational and training purposes. If you need to adapt or modify the materials to tailor them for your audience's needs, go right ahead. We only request that the credit statement found on the copyright page be included on all copies. In addition, if you intend to reproduce the materials in publications for sale or if you wish to use the materials on a large-scale basis (more than one hundred copies in one year), please contact us for prior written permission. Our liberal copyright policy makes it easy and fast for you to use the materials to do your job. Please call us if you have any questions.

Although the *2003 Annuals* are the newest in the series, you will benefit from having the entire series for your use. They are available in paperback and as a three-ring notebook, and the Pfeiffer Library is available on CD-ROM. I personally refer to many of my *Annuals* from the 1980s. They include several classic activities that have become a mainstay in my team-building designs.

But most of all, the *Annuals* have been a valuable resource for over thirty years because the materials come from professionals like you who work in the field as trainers, consultants, facilitators, educators, and performance-improvement technologists. This ensures that the materials have been tried and perfected in real-life settings with actual participants and clients to meet real-world needs. To this end, we encourage you to submit materials to be considered for publication in the *Annual.* At your request we will provide a copy of the guidelines for preparing your materials. We are interested in receiving experiential learning activities (group learning activities based on the five stages of the experiential learning cycle: experiencing, publishing, processing, generalizing, and applying); inventories, questionnaires, and surveys (both paper-and-pencil as well as electronic rating scales); and presentation and discussion resources (articles that may include theory related to practical application). Contact the Jossey-Bass/Pfeiffer Editorial Department at the address listed on the copyright page for copies of our guidelines for contributors or contact me directly at Box 8249, Norfolk, VA 23503 or by email at Pfeiffer-annual@aol.com. We welcome your comments, ideas, and contributions.

Thank you to the dedicated, friendly, thoughtful people at Jossey-Bass/Pfeiffer who produced the *2003 Annuals*: Josh Blatter, Kathleen Dolan Davies, Matt Davis, Dawn Kilgore, Susan Rachmeler, Samya Sattar, and Rebecca Taff. Thank you to Beth Drake of ebb associates inc, who organized this huge task and kept various stages of the submissions flowing in the right directions.

Most important, thank you to our authors, who have once again shared their ideas, techniques, and materials so that HRD professionals everywhere may benefit.

Elaine Biech
Editor
June 2002

About Jossey-Bass/Pfeiffer

Jossey-Bass/Pfeiffer is actively engaged in publishing insightful human resource development (HRD) materials. The organization has earned an international reputation as the leading source of practical resources that are immediately useful to today's consultants, trainers, facilitators, and managers in a variety of industries. All materials are designed by practicing professionals who are continually experimenting with new techniques. Thus, readers and users benefit from the fresh and thoughtful approach that underlies Jossey-Bass/Pfeiffer's experientially based materials, books, workbooks, instruments, and other learning resources and programs. This broad range of products is designed to help human resource practitioners increase individual, group, and organizational effectiveness and provide a variety of training and intervention technologies, as well as background in the field.

CONTENTS

---

*See Experiential Learning Activities Categories, p. 6, for an explanation of the numbering system.

Inventories, Questionnaires, and Surveys

Presentation and Discussion Resources

**Topic is "cutting edge."

GENERAL INTRODUCTION
TO THE 2003 ANNUAL

The 2003 Annual: Volume 2, Consulting is the forty-first volume in the *Annual* series, a collection of practical and useful materials for professionals in the broad area described as human resource development (HRD). The materials are written by and for professionals, including trainers, organization-development and organization-effectiveness consultants, performance-improvement technologists, facilitators, educators, instructional designers, and others.

Each *Annual* has three main sections: experiential learning activities; inventories, questionnaires, and surveys; and presentation and discussion resources. Each published submission is classified in one of the following categories: Individual Development, Communication, Problem Solving, Groups, Teams, Consulting and Facilitating, Leadership, and Organizations. Within each category, pieces are further classified into logical subcategories, which are identified in the introductions to the three sections.

We continue to identify "cutting edge" topics in this *Annual*. This designation highlights topics that present information, concepts, tools, or perspectives that may be recent additions to the profession or that have not previously appeared in the *Annual*.

The series continues to provide an opportunity for HRD professionals who wish to share their experiences, their viewpoints, and their processes with their colleagues. To that end, Jossey-Bass/Pfeiffer publishes guidelines for potential authors. These guidelines are available from the Jossey-Bass/Pfeiffer Editorial Department in San Francisco, California.

Materials are selected for the *Annuals* based on the quality of the ideas, applicability to real-world concerns, relevance to current HRD issues, clarity of presentation, and ability to enhance our readers' professional development. In addition, we choose experiential learning activities that will create a high degree of enthusiasm among the participants and add enjoyment to the learning process. As in the past several years, the contents of each *Annual* span a wide range of subject matter, reflecting the range of interests of our readers.

Our contributor list includes a wide selection of experts in the field: in-house practitioners, consultants, and academically based professionals. A list of contributors to the *Annual* can be found at the end of the volume, including their names, affiliations, addresses, telephone numbers, facsimile numbers, and email addresses. Readers will find this list useful if they wish to locate the authors of specific pieces for feedback, comments, or questions. Further information is presented in a brief biographical sketch of each contributor that appears at the conclusion of each article. We publish this information to encourage "networking," which continues to be a valuable mainstay in the field of human resource development.

We are pleased with the high quality of material that is submitted for publication each year and often regret that we have page limitations. In addition, just as we cannot publish every manuscript we receive, you may find that not all published works are equally useful to you. Therefore, we encourage and invite ideas, materials, and suggestions that will help us to make subsequent *Annuals* as useful as possible to all of our readers.

Introduction
to the Experiential Learning Activities Section

Experiential learning activities ensure that lasting learning occurs. They should be selected with a specific learning objective in mind. These objectives are based on the participants' needs and the facilitator's skills. Although the experiential learning activities presented here all vary in goals, group size, time required, and process,[1] they all incorporate one important element: questions that ensure learning has occurred. This discussion, lead by the facilitator, assists participants to process the activity, to internalize the learning, and to relate it to their day-to-day situations. It is this element that creates the unique experience and learning opportunity that only an experiential learning activity can bring to the group process.

Readers have used the *Annuals'* experiential learning activities for years to enhance their training and consulting events. Each learning experience is complete and includes all lecturettes, handout content, and other written material necessary to facilitate the activity. In addition, many include variations of the design that the facilitator might find useful. If the activity does not fit perfectly with your objective, within your time frame, or to your group size, we encourage you to adapt the activity by adding your own variations. You will find additional experiential learning activities listed in the "Experiential Learning Activities Categories" chart that immediately follows this introduction.

The 2003 Annual: Volume 2, Consulting includes thirteen activities, in the following categories:

---

[1]It would be redundant to print here a caveat for the use of experiential learning activities, but HRD professionals who are not experienced in the use of this training technology are strongly urged to read the "Introduction" to the *Reference Guide to Handbooks and Annuals* (1999 Edition). This article presents the theory behind the experiential-learning cycle and explains the necessity of adequately completing each phase of the cycle to allow effective learning to occur.

Locate other activities in these and other categories in the "Experiential Learning Activities Categories" chart that follows, or the comprehensive *Reference Guide to Handbooks and Annuals*. This book, which is updated regularly, indexes all of the *Annuals* and all of the *Handbooks of Structured Experiences* that we have published to date. With each revision, the *Reference Guide* becomes a complete, up-to-date, and easy-to-use resource for selecting appropriate materials from all of the *Annuals* and *Handbooks*. A print version of the *Reference Guide* is available for volumes through 1999. An online supplement covering the years through 2003 can be found at www.pfeiffer.com/go/supplement.

EXPERIENTIAL LEARNING ACTIVITIES CATEGORIES

740. What *You* See:
Examining Different Points of View

Goals

- To experience that we filter and organize elements of experience in line with what is personally important to us.

- To recognize that we all selectively encounter and record experiences.

- To understand that others with whom we share a common space perceive differing dimensions of it.

- To learn that different perspectives can serve as a basis for conflict.

Group Size

A maximum of forty individuals seated at round tables in groups of no more than eight. This works best if people live or work together.

Time Required

Approximately one hour, depending on differences among and number of people.

Materials

- The What You See Lecturette for the facilitator.

- A sheet of blank paper for each participant.

- A pen or pencil for each participant.

- Flip chart and felt-tipped markers or an overhead projector and transparency sheets and markers.

- A timing device.

Physical Setting

A room that comfortably seats groups of five to eight at round tables. The surface and lighting should be sufficient for map drawing and the room should permit individuals to hear each other without microphones.

Process

1. Do not identify the goals of the activity prior to the completion of the process. Do not introduce the activity with a discussion of diversity.

2. Ask participants to form groups of from five to eight who know one another and work together, if this is possible. Hand out blank sheets of paper, one to each person, along with a pencil or pen. Ask the participants to draw a map of a space they all encounter regularly, a space with which they are all familiar (each group can choose what to draw, for example, the campus, the plant, or the department in which they work). Instruct them not to start until you say go and that they will have five minutes to draw the map. They may not talk with anyone nor use materials. Do not ask if there are questions. Ask if they are ready—if they all have a pencil that works and paper. If they ask questions about what kind of map is desired or about the space to be mapped, do not respond. Just repeat: "Draw a map of 'X.' You have five minutes."

   Note: Do not give them too long to draw the maps. The longer the time, the more they will feel required to make the maps approximate an "objective" transportation guide. (Ten minutes.)

3. When the time has passed, announce: "Time is up." Ask individuals within each group to share their maps and discuss what they notice about each map. (Individuals might be different in their work roles, ages, where they live, social class, or any other dimension that could affect their experience with the space they see.) (Ten minutes.)

4. Facilitate a reporting out of the main discussion points for the total group. They should see similarities and differences and they should see that the differences reflect the details of their distinctive experiences with the space (where their office is located, how long they have functioned in the space, where they live, their mode of transportation to the space, etc.) Ask questions such as:

   ■ What distinguishes the maps from one another?

   ■ Why do people see the same thing in different ways?

- In what ways do our prior experiences and our present positions influence what we see?

(Fifteen minutes.)

5. Deliver the What You See Lecturette. When you are finished, ask questions such as:

- Based on what you have just heard, what other insights do you have about why you each experience the same space differently?
- What factors might lead to different experiences with the space? (For example, commuter students tend to draw maps of campuses that emphasize roads, parking lots, and the buildings they use. Residential students tend to draw maps that emphasize walkways or buildings between the dorms and their classrooms. New students show maps with less detail than do advanced students. People who live in inner cities often show public transportation stops while those who live in suburbs show highways when drawing the same city.)
- How might different perspectives affect our interactions within a space?
- What have you learned about each other that you can use when working together in the future?
- In what ways will you act differently with one another?
- What can we generalize from this experience?

(Fifteen minutes.)

Submitted by Anne M. McMahon and C. Louise Sellaro.

Anne M. McMahon, Ph.D., is a professor of management at Youngstown State University, organizer for the Partners for Workplace Diversity initiative with Youngstown area employers, and a member of the National Workplace Diversity Committee of the Society for Human Resource Management. She has published in several interdisciplinary journals.

C. Louise Sellaro, D.B.A., is a professor of management at Youngstown State University, Youngstown, Ohio. She teaches and has published teaching cases in the area of strategic leadership. She works with Partners for Workplace Diversity and is an active member of the nationwide organization, Initiative for Competitive Inner Cities (ICIC). She also does consulting related to program development focused on education of the disadvantaged.

What You See Lecturette

Everyday experience is always a complex, nearly overwhelming set of sights, sounds, shapes, and movements. Since people try to affect what happens to them, they attend to what is going on. So much is going on and there are so many details that make up any experience that much of it is not relevant to the person, who then filters out some of the details and organizes the rest in a way that enables him or her to understand the experience in terms of what is important to him or her. People ignore some sights, movements, sounds, and the like, focusing on others. Two individuals acting in the same "objective setting" will recognize different dimensions in the experience, organize them differently, and remember them differently because they do not share the same perspective on the setting. That is, they encounter the specifics differently because they never occupy the same space in the setting, for example, one person is at the front of the room or acting in one role while another is at the back of the room acting in another role. They are in the same "objective setting," but encounter different sights and sounds and their roles sensitize them to other differences.

Memories are representations of a person's experiences. If individuals see an experience as a "repeated version" of an earlier one, their representation of it will be somewhat "generalized," but only within the range of their own personal experiences. Thus, each individual forms cognitive views of his or her experiences that are always representative of personal interactions with the world. In other words, the world is always more complex than any one person's representation of it.

People tend to presume that their remembered representations are accurate, faithful, objective records of what happened. People later use what they remember as accurate. They form expectations of what will, can, and should happen as well as what things mean. Moreover, they are likely to presume that others in the setting have a vision of the experience very similar to their own. This is particularly so when an interaction goes well and when the setting is repeated.

The presumption that other individuals enter an experience with similar cognitive perspectives can create serious difficulties for our interactions. When differences do emerge, they are likely to be seen as issues of "reality contact" or "right and wrong." When differences in perspectives overlap demographic differences, such as age, race, or time on the job, inferences are often made about the demographic group associated with the difference (for example, "You know how young people are today" or "She's ready for the golden parachute"). Thus, understanding that all individuals enter an experience with different cognitive perspectives is a key diversity awareness. That is, an individual who perceives another as similar ought never to conclude that they both share a similar perspective as they continue to interact. Coping with differences in perspectives effectively is a basic diversity competence.

741. EARLY MEMORIES: LEARNING ABOUT STEREOTYPES*

Goals

- To open a discussion on racism in American society.
- To reduce defensiveness on the part of participants when discussing racism.
- To recognize that attitudes about race are developed very early in childhood and are not forgotten.
- To open a discussion on management of unconscious attitudes and stereotypes.

Group Size

Up to thirty participants as racially balanced as possible, who know and trust one another relatively well.

Time Required

Approximately one hour.

Materials

- One copy of the Early Memories Lecturette for the facilitator.
- A flip chart and felt-tipped markers.

---

*Note: This activity should not be used until the group has built a level of trust with one another. This activity is effective in discussing race in the United States and is not applicable to adults who have grown up in other countries or cultures.

Physical Setting

Participants need adequate room to pair off and discuss issues without over-hearing one another.

Trainer's Note

While often uncomfortable for participants, this activity can permit partici-pants to recognize that having stereotypes about others is universal human behavior and is nothing to be ashamed of. Only when stereotyping is raised to a conscious level, however, can we effectively change our behavior and reac-tions. The goal is to bring the participants to a point at which the desire to deny or minimize the impact of racism in our society is replaced by an under-standing that racism is, in fact, deeply embedded in our national psyche. In accepting this fact, participants can recognize the universality of their experi-ence, de-personalize it, and begin to explore its implications for their current attitudes and beliefs.

Process

1. After stating the goals of the activity, begin by delivering the Early Memo-ries Lecturette to the group. (Five minutes.)

2. Ask the group to form pairs of mixed race. If necessary, it is possible to use triads. Do not go larger than triads.

3. Once the group is paired up, ask the participants to be silent and to re-flect on the following question: "Go to your very earliest memory or un-derstanding about race. This may be your first understanding about what race you are, or what race others are. Find the first memory you can— when you realized there was a difference. What is that memory?" Let the group reflect in silence. (Five minutes.)

4. Call time and ask the pairs to face each other and share their memories with one another. (Ten minutes.)

5. After the ten minutes, recognize for the group that this may have been an emotional or difficult experience for some participants. Say, "Conversa-tions about race are risky and loaded with unresolved emotions. You may have found this conversation very difficult, but I congratulate you on tak-ing the risk, because it is by engaging in these kinds of discussions that we experience the greatest understanding of others and personal growth."

6. Ask the group to think about the following question silently: "When you first became aware of race in the incident you remembered, did you have a sense of which race you *perceived* it was better to be?" (Be very careful to use the word perceived, as there should be no implication that there is actually a "better" race to be.) (Two minutes.)

7. After allowing them to reflect for a few minutes, ask people whether they did have such a perception. Usually, there will be general assent from the participants that they had a perception of which it was "better" to be. Ask how young they were at the time of their memory. People may volunteer to answer this question. (Five minutes.)

8. Ask the following questions:

   - How early in life were your views about race formed?

   - What was the impact of your gaining some perception of race at an early age?

   (Ten minutes.)

9. Discuss their answers, making the following points: (a) It is perfectly normal human behavior to hold stereotypes and (b) only after we have acknowledged this natural behavior can we begin to manage our reactions and behaviors on the emotional issue of race. (Ten minutes.)

10. Use the group's understanding of the points above as a stepping off point to further explore the issues of race, stereotypes, and personal responsibility. Participants may wish to make a list of actions to take or mantras to remember about racism and stereotyping.

Variation

- Use with other ethnic groups, religions, or genders if desired.

Submitted by Renée Yuengling.

Renée Yuengling is the managing partner of the Whitman Group, Inc. and can be reached at whitmangroup@earthlink.net. Ms. Yuengling specializes in diversity and intercultural coaching for executives. She is a specialist in the area of multicultural leadership and works with the U.S military on cross-cultural leadership and followership issues.

Early Memories Lecturette**

"I'm colorblind."

"I don't notice what color someone is."

"I'm not racist."

"You don't really think racism is still a problem do you? Didn't we solve that in the Sixties?"

"Oh, I don't have any stereotypes about people. I really don't think that way."

How many times have we heard a well-meaning person make one of the comments above? Individuals who make these claims do so in all earnestness, believing themselves to have risen above or never to have acquired the ugly stereotypes that populate our modern lives. The reality, of course, is that stereotypes reside deep in our subconscious, are a universal human behavior, and are impossible to remove once acquired. They can only be managed through awareness of them.

Talking about race in America is fraught with danger and fear. Most of us would prefer to think the racial divide was bridged in the 1960s and all that is asked of us today is not to "behave" in racist ways. The thought of discussing bigotry and prejudice in a racially mixed group can produce extreme anxiety.

Often, the greatest reticence to engage in an honest discussion about race can come from European-Americans, but it can be difficult for African-Americans as well. For European-Americans, it is easy to accept the notion that there is no longer a racial problem in the United States and that African-Americans may be simply "too sensitive." European-Americans often seem bewildered when confronted with the racism experienced by others, although they may have experienced ethnic stereotyping themselves. And many are surprised and defensive when African-Americans react with anger at their bewilderment. But their bewilderment is not always counterfeit. After all, European-Americans generally are not touched by racism; they probably don't experience racism in day-to-day life or recognize it for what it is when they do see it. Because European-Americans usually do not experience racism and aren't required to cope with it, they may assume that, if it doesn't exist for them, it doesn't exist. African-Americans, on the other hand, are on the receiving end of lingering racism in America and must cope with it on a daily

---

**Note:* The terms European-American and African-American are used to connote individuals who have grown up in the United States and who are of either European or African heritage.

basis. Such widely divergent experiences create many of the misunderstand-ings and much of the anger that can arise in any discussion of race.

Americans live in a society so permeated by our history of racism that it is probably not possible to be truly "colorblind," nor is it really desirable. The goal of this activity is simply to recognize that we all have prejudices held deeply in our subconscious that were imprinted early in our childhoods.

To say "I don't notice what color someone is" may really mean you haven't examined your own attitudes about it. Only through personal reflec-tion can we recognize societal influences on our understanding of race. Once we realize that it is impossible to escape these influences, then and only then are we ready to do the necessary personal work to understand and manage the influences and the stereotypes we ourselves hold.

We will learn today the extent to which we were taught at a very early age what we still subconsciously believe. This activity also serves as a call to you as individuals to accept the difficult truth of our humanity: It is natural and normal to harbor stereotypes about others. All people in all cultures have them. What is important is to understand what stereotypes we hold, to examine them, and to manage them according to our personal values.

742. Blind Soccer Game: Following the Leader

Goals

- To demonstrate the importance of clear communication between leaders and their workers.
- To demonstrate the importance of the whole group (team) of people understanding the direction (goal), versus only the leader (coach) understanding.

Group Size

Ten to twenty participants.

Time Required

Forty-five to sixty minutes.

Materials

- One small size soccer ball.
- Blindfolds, one for each participant.
- Four orange cones (used by children's basketball or soccer teams).

Physical Setting

This activity can be conducted indoors or outdoors. The optimal area is approximately fifty feet wide by one hundred feet long without any plate glass windows or patio doors or other breakable objects.

Process

1. Explain that they will be doing a physical activity, but that it does not require athletic prowess and will not be physically demanding.

2. Set two orange cones approximately ten to fifteen feet apart at one end of the space and two more orange cones the same distance apart at the other end of the available space (approximately eighty to one hundred feet away). Say that the cones represent the goals through which the teams will try to kick a soccer ball.

3. Divide the participants into two teams at random. Have each team choose or appoint one member as the team's coach.

4. Give the blindfolds to the two coaches and have them distribute one blindfold to each player. The coaches will not wear blindfolds.

5. Have the players place the blindfolds on themselves. The blindfolds should be tight enough to prevent the players from seeing the playing field, other players, and the goals for their teams.

6. Have the coaches assist each of their players onto the "playing field." Tell the coaches to agree on which goal belongs to which team.

7. Explain to everyone that they can only move when instructed to do so by their own coach. Coaches may walk around the playing field but may not touch the players. They may only use verbal commands to describe who may move, where to move, and when to kick the ball.

8. Begin the game. Be prepared to have the ball kicked everywhere but at the appropriate goal. If the ball is kicked too far from the players, retrieve it and place it next to the closest player. (Ten minutes.)

9. After five to ten minutes of play, stop the game. Have all the players remove their blindfolds and discuss the experience with the group, asking the following:

   ■ How well did your coach give instructions to all players on your team?

   ■ What were the positives and negatives of having only the coaches know what was going on?

   ■ How frustrated were coaches with the situation?

   ■ What happened when you were solely responsible for knowing the team's goal?

   ■ How is this situation analogous to others in your life?

   (Fifteen minutes.)

10. Now blindfold the coaches. Have a few members of each team gently spin their coach around for five to six revolutions and then spin him or her in the opposite direction.

11. Inform the teams that they will participate again in a mock soccer game. Just as in the first game, the team will need to wait for instructions from their coach. This time, however, the players will be sure of where their goal is located. The players must communicate to their blindfolded coaches where the soccer ball is at any given time and where the nearest player is located. The players may not move until they have received instructions from their respective coaches.

12. Start the new game and observe what happens. (Five to ten minutes.)

13. Bring the group together again for discussion of the following questions:

   - Did the second game result in more scoring? Why do you think that was?

   - Is it better for players to see the goal or for the coach to see the goal? (It should be obvious that when players are able to see the goal, they can provide more information to the coach, who in turn can provide more information to the players, who in turn can make faster decisions, positively impacting the scoring of a goal.)

   - How can what you have learned through this experience help you work in groups back on the job?

   - If you are leading a group or task force, what would you do to assure that the members of your group could "score" successfully?

   - If you were a member of such a group, what steps could you take to aim for the proper goal if you were confused or "blindfolded"?

   (Twenty minutes.)

14. Write plans of action on the flip chart that participants have agreed to implement back on the job. (Five minutes.)

Variations

- Groups larger than twenty people can participate in this activity. The extra team members might be used to line the perimeter of the makeshift soccer field and take notes for the discussion. Each group can experience being blindfolded while trying to reach a goal.

- Intact work groups can be placed on the same teams and later discussion can center on how the activity was similar to what actually occurs on the job.

Submitted by Brad Humphrey and Jeff Stokes.

Brad Humphrey is one of the co-founders of Pinnacle Performance Group, leadership improvement specialists. The company provides training and consulting in strategic planning, leadership, project management, process and system analysis, problem solving, continuous improvement, sales, and customer service. He is also the co-author of The 21st Century Supervisor *and has helped to develop an excellent training course for front-line leaders by the same name. He speaks all over the world, assisting organizations in every industry.*

Jeff Stokes is a co-founder of Pinnacle Performance Group, leadership improvement specialists. The company provides training and consulting in strategic planning, leadership, project management, process and system analysis, problem solving, continuous improvement, sales, and customer service. He is also co-author of The 21st Century Supervisor *and has helped to develop an excellent training course for front-line leaders by the same name. Stokes speaks all over the world, assisting organizations in every industry.*

743. A FINE PREDICAMENT: CHECKING EXPECTATIONS OF OTHERS

Goals

- To provide team-building opportunities using a process of inquiry while having fun getting to know co-workers and teammates better.

- To learn to listen more critically, argue our cases more convincingly, and understand others' points of view through dialogue.

- To make a distinction between our expectations of others and the conclusions we make about them that support or defy those expectations.

- To differentiate what we already know about others from what we learn about them.

- To examine our ability to predict others' thoughts, words, and decisions.

Group Size

Twelve participants from an intact work team.

Time Required

One and one-half hours.

Materials

- One "Scruples®: Millennium Edition" game, which can be purchased at most large toy stores or online at www.amazon.com or www.escape.ca/~scruples/.

- Prepared overhead transparency or flip-chart sheet of the A Fine Predicament Game Objectives.

- Prepared overhead transparency or flip-chart sheet of A Fine Predicament Card Descriptions.

- Prepared overhead transparency or flip-chart sheet of A Fine Predicament Play Guidelines.

- Blank paper and pencils for each participant.

- A timing device.

Physical Setting

A room set up for three teams of four participants each to work in "quads." Round or square tables are best, but rectangular tables can be adjoined width-side to width-side to form a square.

Process*

1. Introduce the goals of the session.

2. Form groups of four players and seat them at tables facing one another so that their cards will not be visible to other players. Explain that they will be playing a game called Scruples. Display the A Fine Predicament Game Objectives and describe the general objectives of the game by saying: "In this game, players (Questioners) take turns choosing another player at the table (the Answerer) whom they think would respond to a situation in a way that matches the response card the Questioner has drawn. For each match the Questioner makes, he or she earns one point. Incorrect matches earn no points. The winner of the game is the person who earns the most points." Answer any questions participants may have at this point. (Ten minutes.)

3. For each group of four players, place twelve Scruples Red Reply Cards face-down in the center of the table. Randomly distribute three Scruples Dilemma Cards to each player, asking them not to share what is written on the cards with their tablemates. Also, give each player one Scruples Ballot Card. (Five minutes.)

4. Display the A Fine Predicament Card Descriptions and raise a sample of each type of card in turn and explain: "Yellow Dilemma Cards pose ethical dilemmas. Red Reply Cards specify the answer that the Questioner

---

*Note that the process described here is an adaptation of the original rules of Scruples® intended to save time and allow for more discussion following the game.

is seeking from the Answerer. There are three possible answers, 'Yes,' 'No,' and 'It Depends.' The Ballot Cards have two sides—a halo on one side and a pitchfork on the other. In the event that a Questioner does not believe the Answerer's response to the Dilemma Card, all players vote whether the Answerer would, in reality, do what the Questioner thought in response to the dilemma posed.

5. Illustrate the play of the game by the following example while showing A Fine Predicament Play Guidelines. Hand yellow Dilemma Card #185 to any one of the four players in a quad (Scruples cards are numbered in the lower right-hand corner). Explain by saying, "In this game, players take turns as 'Questioners,' asking ethical dilemma questions of another player (the Answerer) in hopes of getting the answer they're looking for." (Five minutes.)

6. Give the Questioner a red Reply Card that reads "Yes," but ask him or her not to share it with anyone else. Then instruct the Questioner to ask the question on Card #185 ("Guests are due when your dog snatches the turkey and drags it out the door. Do you retrieve and serve it?") of any other player in the quad (the Answerer) whom he or she believes will provide the answer specified on the Reply Card that he or she has drawn. Explain by saying, "Since Questioners are trying to get a match between the word printed on the Reply Card they drew just prior to their turn (yes, no, or it depends) and what the Answerer actually responds, the game involves asking the question on the Dilemma Card of the one other player whom you believe is *most likely* to respond with the word listed on the Reply Card." Clarify if required. (Two minutes.)

7. Now ask the Answerer to answer the question "yes," "no," or "it depends" (in which case the person has to give a brief explanation of why it depends). Say, "If the Reply Card and the response match, the questioner earns one point." (Two minutes.)

8. Tell the Questioner to say whether or not a point was earned. If so, discard the yellow Dilemma Card. Play then moves clockwise to the next player, who reads the dilemma on his or her yellow Dilemma Card and picks the player whose answer he or she thinks would match that on the Reply Card he or she has drawn. Explain what happens if the answer does not match by saying, "Of course, the Questioner might not get the answer he is looking for from the Answerer, in which case the Questioner can choose not to pursue the issue further, and lose the point, or challenge the issue, which brings us to 'Ballot Cards.'" (Two minutes.)

9. Explain Scruples Ballot Cards by saying, "Let's say that the Answerer says she would not serve the turkey, but the Questioner believes she would in fact do so. To challenge, the Questioner announces that he or she thinks the Answerer is bluffing. The Questioner then has twenty seconds to convince the other two players in the group that the Answerer is bluffing, citing evidence from the Answerer's disposition, temperament, or past behavior." (Two minutes.)

10. For the sake of the example, ask the Questioner to play along and make a twenty-second argument that the Answerer would, in reality, serve the turkey after all. Explain by saying, "The Answerer then has twenty seconds to convince the other players that he or she is telling the truth and would not serve the turkey." Ask the Answerer to defend his or her answer. (Two minutes.)

11. Explain by saying, "The winner of the challenge is decided by a vote. The Answerer's sincerity is determined by a simultaneous vote in which all four players individually (including the Questioner and the Answerer) hold up the halo side of the Ballot Card if they think the Answerer is sincere, or the pitchfork side if they think it's a bluff." Clarify if necessary. (Two minutes.)

12. Ask all players in the quad to hold up the halo side of their Ballot Cards if they think the Answerer is sincere, or the pitchfork side if they think he or she is bluffing. Tally up the votes. Explain by saying, "If the Questioner wins the challenge, he or she earns the point. If the Answerer wins the challenge, he or she does. In the event of a tie vote, the Answerer earns the point. In any case, the Questioner discards the yellow Dilemma Card and draws a new red Reply Card that he or she keeps secret. Play then continues clockwise to the next player, who asks his or her Dilemma Card question of any other player. This process repeats until all questions have been asked, at which time the winner of the game (or winners, if players tie for points) is announced." (Two minutes.)

13. Ask if there are any questions regarding the process of play, then announce the following play guidelines: "Keep Dilemma Cards and Reply Cards face-down for the time being. You already have your Ballot Cards, which you keep throughout the game. Decide among your quad which player starts first and proceed in a clockwise fashion. Make use of challenges! Lively discussion is the ultimate goal of the game. Challenging makes the game more fun and provides some teachable moments as well." (Two minutes.)

14. Ask if there are any remaining questions and announce that you (the facilitator) will be circulating around the room to troubleshoot. Instruct participants that they have the next thirty minutes to play the game. Start a timer and then circulate among the tables. (Thirty minutes.)

15. After participants have used all of their yellow Dilemma Cards (or the time has expired), debrief the game with the following questions:

   - As Questioner, what influenced your decision when picking whom to ask a Dilemma question of? (*Teaching point:* There's no shame in being wrong in your expectations; better to formulate a reasonable expectation based on what you know about a person and be wrong than to ask questions randomly and stumble on the answer you're looking for.)

   - In situations where "It Depends" was the answer actually given by the Answerer, were you as Questioner surprised by the rationale given? (*Teaching point:* As we don't know what the Answerer would do if his or her dog had dragged a frozen turkey from the kitchen *before it was cooked,* thus, our expectations are limited when we don't consider the influence other people, places, times, and circumstances might have on a situation.)

   - The questions and answers asked in the game are clearly of the "what if" variety. How much confidence do you have that the answers you received to your questions accurately reflect what people would do in a given situation? (*Teaching point:* There are no right answers in this game. Just because an Answerer supported or refuted the Questioner's Reply Card doesn't mean the Answerer's response was truthful. Only the Answerer [and perhaps not even that person] knows how he or she would really behave in the ethical dilemma presented. Such is often the case in our dealings with others—we don't know with absolute certainty that our findings are "true" or "facts.")

   - Were you ever challenged by another player and lost the vote, even though you were telling the truth? How did it feel? (*Teaching point:* The old maxim of the tyranny of the majority holds that everybody can agree and still be wrong.)

   - Did you ever bluff, bend the truth, or just plain lie as an Answerer? What are the dangers of doing this in a work setting? (*Teaching point:* Bluffing about something you have done in the past requires you to make even more elaborate lies to patch holes in your story. Bluffing about what you would do in the future might be dangerous in that others develop expectations regarding your behavior that you may or may not be willing or able to live up to.)

- How can you use what you have learned from playing the game—about yourself and about others in the group—when you return to the workplace?

(Twenty minutes.)

Variations

- If there are fewer than twelve participants, divide into groups with one or two teams of three participants as necessary. For teams smaller than four participants, distribute three Dilemma Cards and three Reply Cards to each player.
- If there are more than twelve participants, purchase another Scruples game so that there is one box for each twelve participants, two boxes for thirteen to twenty-four participants, etc.
- Some questions presented on the Dilemma Cards may be too sensitive for some groups. The following card numbers from the Millennium Edition are recommended for play among business colleagues or students in a classroom (cards are numbered in the lower right corner): 4, 8, 10, 20, 22, 37, 39, 44, 53, 56, 60, 66, 67, 74, 76, 81, 84, 87, 91, 92, 93, 100, 103, 105, 107, 109, 110, 112, 116, 117, 119, 124, 125, 127, 129, 132, 133, 138, 139, 141, 143, 145, 147, 156, 160, 176, 177, 188, 190, 196, 200, 201, 205, 208, 211, 215, 223, 224, 227, 228, 235, 240, 242, 244, 246, 248.
- Rather than using the Dilemma Cards included with the game, you can make up your own. For example, for a business audience you might make up a card reading "There are unsubstantiated—but perhaps true—rumors going around the office that a new employee has recently been in prison for a tax evasion charge. Do you ask him if it's true?"

Submitted by Doug Leigh.

Doug Leigh, Ph.D., *earned his doctorate in instructional systems from Florida State University and is an assistant professor of organizational leadership with Pepperdine University's Graduate School of Education. He is a co-author of* Useful Education Results *with Roger Kaufman and Ryan Watkins (Proactive Publications) and frequently contributes to professional publications and conferences regarding the topics of needs assessment, strategic planning, evaluation, SWOT analysis, and data-based decision making.*

A FINE PREDICAMENT GAME OBJECTIVES

- In this game, players (as Questioners) take turns trying to match the response they see on a Reply Card they have drawn with the actual answer given by another player (the Answerer).

- Each match made is worth one point. No points are earned if answers do not match.

- The winner of the game is the player who earns the most points.

A Fine Predicament Card Descriptions

Dilemma Cards

- These cards pose ethical dilemmas.

- Each player starts the game with three yellow Dilemma Cards and discards each after the question is asked.

Reply Cards

- These cards specify the answer that the Questioner is seeking of the Answerer.

- There are three possible answers: "yes," "no," and "it depends."

- Questioners draw Reply Cards just prior to their turn and discard them after their turn is over.

Ballot Cards

- Used by all players in the event of a challenge by the Questioner to vote whether the Answerer would, in reality, act as he or she responded to the dilemma posed by the Questioner.

The 2003 Annual: Volume 2, Consulting/© 2003 John Wiley & Sons, Inc.

A Fine Predicament Play Guidelines

- Decide among your group which player goes first and proceed in a clockwise fashion.

- Make use of challenges! Lively discussion is the ultimate goal of the game. Challenging makes the game more fun and provides some teachable moments as well.

- Don't be reluctant to bluff.

- Keep track of the number of points each person has earned.

- Please return all cards at the end of the game.

744. Decision Making: Voting with Your Feet*

Goals

- To perform a quick assessment of group views on one or several issues.

- To allow a group to share views, opinions, abilities, or interests easily with one another.

- To energize participants in a classroom or group meeting.

Group Size

Two to two hundred.

Time Required

Thirty to forty minutes, including a short break.

Materials

- Overhead transparency or flip-chart sheet with voting directions prepared in advance, as shown in Step 3.

- A flip chart listing of issues to be reviewed or flip-chart space for the group to generate them.

- A flip-chart easel with plenty of paper or an overhead projector and transparency film.

- Markers (appropriate for the medium).

- Masking tape.

---

*We provide this piece as a service for newer group leaders. It is not, strictly speaking, an experiential learning activity, but we believe it to be a highly useful technique for polling a group.

Physical Setting

Room for all participants to stand and move about easily. Sufficient gathering space on the right, left, and middle portions of the room to put up easels or post sheets on the wall.

Trainer's Note

Sometimes a team or group has reached an impasse or a point at which they are talking around a decision but are unable to make it. Physical movement may help them to break through the barrier.

Process

1. Post a controversial issue or decision options that the group has previously generated. These can be recorded on a flip chart or a blank transparency.

2. Explain to the group members that they are not making a final decision through this process, but that it is a way to see how people stand on the issue right now.

3. Explain the ratings and post the flip-chart sheet you prepared in advance, as shown below. Point out and verbally label the left, center, and right sides of the room as the "yes," "neutral," and "no" zones. If desired, hang a piece of chart paper to identify each. (Five minutes.)

Yes ◄──────────── **Neutral** ────────────► **No**

4. Ask participants to stand and move to the area classifying their vote on the issue in question. (Five minutes.)

5. Count the people in each area. Call out the results and record them where all can see. Lead a discussion of the meaning of the ratings, if needed. (Ten minutes.)

6. Ask everyone to take a ten-minute break. (Ten minutes.)

7. When everyone returns, summarize what happened and ask whether people have any new thoughts or would like to change their positions. Lead a discussion of the new thoughts and ask again for a final decision. (Ten minutes.)

Variations

- The ratings can be used to determine: Where do we go from here?

- A series of quick, playful yes-no questions can be used as a warm-up, such as "Who likes broccoli?"

- Rather than having only three possible "votes," there can be a scale from 1 to 5 or 1 to 10. If most people are clustered above or below the middle, this is a discussion point.

- Nominal categories, such as being aware of the concept, using the concept, or being ready to teach others, can be used.

- Use a sketch of a plan on a flip chart and ask participants to go "stand by their plan"—that is, what they are willing to do.

- In Step 4 above, participants may raise their hands for "yes," turn thumbs down for "no," and cross their arms for "neutral." This adaptation accommodates a larger audience or works even if space is too limited to move about.

- As a variation on recording, take a photograph of the human array, or have people write their names on the chart and/or overhead transparency.

Submitted by M.K. Key.

M.K. Key, Ph.D., is a clinical-community psychologist and the founder of Key Associates, LLC, in Nashville, Tennessee. She is a nationally recognized speaker on leadership, releasing the creative spirit, mediation of conflict, and team development. She has authored over thirty publications on such topics as change management, continuous quality improvement, strategic business issues, and leadership during turbulent times. She also serves as adjunct professor of organization and human development at Vanderbilt University.

745. Art Appreciation: Taking a Field Trip

Goals

- To encourage self-disclosure and develop greater awareness of the goals, backgrounds, preferences, and personalities of individual team members.

- To develop a more cohesive team through a consensus choice team-building activity.

- To expose participants to an experience of art and one or more cultural institutions in their community.

Group Size

Ten or fewer members of an intact work group.

Time Required

Depending on the size of the group, one hour and fifteen to one hour and forty minutes, in addition to travel time to and from the site.

Materials

- Small notepads and pens or pencils for each participant.
- Flip chart and markers for debriefing (optional).
- Postcard, poster, or other souvenir for each participant (optional).

Physical Setting

An art museum or other cultural institution in your community or at the site where your team-building retreat or conference is being held.

Preparation

Check to see whether any team members serve on the board or are otherwise involved with an institution. If possible, choose an exhibit or collection that would be new to most of your participants. Check with the museum to find a time when it is likely to be less crowded and not conflict with scheduled tours or docents. Be sure that you have discussed this activity, including the goals and purpose, with appropriate museum staff.

Process

1. Gather the group together at your base site, or meet outside of the museum if desired, and distribute small notebooks and pens or pencils to all participants. Explain: "This is a team-building field trip." Describe your goals for the event and encourage the group to enjoy the experience, keep an open mind, and participate fully.

2. Bring the group into the pre-selected exhibit area and describe the task: "Please walk through the exhibit quietly on your own. Look at every piece of art, sculpture, or whatever is on display. Your task is to choose at least *one image* (which can be all or part of a work of art) that you *personally* identify with, in one of the following ways:

   - An image that speaks to or symbolizes *who you are today*.

   - An image that speaks to or symbolizes an *important event or milestone* in your life.

   - An image that speaks to or symbolizes a *challenge you have faced* or are facing.

   - An image that speaks to or symbolizes *who you are becoming*.

   Jot down the image and any thoughts or notes on your notepad." (Ten minutes.)

3. Tell them they will have fifteen minutes and let everyone go to work. Gather the group together at the end of fifteen minutes. Ask how they did on the task, in general, and take comments on the exhibit or the process. (Fifteen minutes for the project and a few minutes for discussion.)

4. Then ask one member at a time to volunteer to describe his or her choice of a visual metaphor. One at a time, they are to lead the entire group, as a docent would, to the front of their chosen works of art and point out and discuss the images, answering questions about why they chose the pieces.

Encourage other group members to ask questions to better understand the meaning of each individual's choice or metaphor. For example, "I chose the picture of Monet's Water Lilies, because I have been trying to become more calm and peaceful, and when I look at them, I feel that way" or "I spent a year abroad in France and the images make me remember a different, less stressful kind of lifestyle." Give all members the opportunity to become the "docent." (Allow someone to "pass" if for any reason he or she feels uncomfortable and doesn't want to share.) (Up to five minutes per person: One to two minutes for sharing, plus two or three minutes for clarification.)

5. When all members have had the opportunity to share their metaphors, ask the group as a whole, "So what have you learned about your team and team members?" You may hear things like "We all like bright colors" or "We seem to enjoy humorous pieces" or comments about individual team members. If time allows, take a few comments from each person in turn.

6. The final task will be for the group to choose, by consensus, one image that best personifies either:

   ■ Who they are as a team or organization or

   ■ Where they are going as a team or organization.

   Document the team's choice and discuss the process of making the choice. (Five to ten minutes.)

7. Reconvene the group either back at your site or outside for a debriefing to discuss the following:

   ■ What surprised you about this experience?

   ■ What did you learn about yourself?

   ■ What did we learn about our team?

   ■ How can we use our metaphor/symbol to remind us of our focus and direction in the future?

   If possible, write these answers on a flip chart. (Ten minutes.)

8. Conclude the activity and distribute a postcard, poster, or small souvenir from the museum. If your team building is going to continue, segue learnings and the team's choice of image into the remainder of your session.

Submitted by Donna L. Goldstein.

Donna L. Goldstein, Ph.D., *is managing director of Development Associates International, a management consulting and training firm in Hollywood, Florida. Dr. Goldstein and her colleagues have helped over 275 organizations worldwide to create happier staffs, healthier teams, and more productive and profitable workforces. She holds a doctorate in human resource development from Florida International University. She has contributed to fourteen books on HR and OD, including McGraw-Hill's* Training and Performance Sourcebooks.

746. Teams by Any Other Name: Examining Team Values

Goals

- To provide a challenging and pleasant activity to help generate team spirit among members of an intact team.

- To provide participants an opportunity to examine new ways to look at teamwork.

- To generate team spirit among all participants.

Group Size

Any size grouped in intact work teams.

Time Required

One hour to one hour and ten minutes.

Materials

- One Teams by Any Other Name Metaphors Listing for each participant.

- One Teams by Any Other Name Leadership Traits Listing for each participant (for the Variation).

- Paper (optional) and a pencil or pen for each participant.

- A flip chart and felt-tipped markers.

Physical Setting

A room arranged with tables that will seat the intact teams. Six-foot rectangular tables or round tables work well.

Process

1. Have people seat themselves at the tables in their regular work groups and give everyone blank paper and a pen or pencil. Briefly explain that each of the groups will be working with a variety of metaphors to discover new understandings about their team in particular and about teamwork in the workplace in general. (Two minutes.)

2. Next give everyone a copy of the Teams by Any Other Name Metaphors Listing and read through the directions. Write one example on the flip chart and clarify if necessary. (Five minutes.)

3. Tell people to first fill out the worksheet individually. Say that they will have five minutes to do so. (Five minutes.)

4. Call time and have work group members share what they have written with one another, explaining why they chose the noun they did and why they felt their metaphors were appropriate. Remind members of the groups to really listen to what others are saying. (Fifteen minutes.)

5. Ask each group to select a spokesperson to share what they discovered with the large group. Take five minutes for them to share before continuing to work. (Five minutes.)

6. Now have the teams regroup and identify what they would like to retain from their own metaphors as well as the metaphors that others on their team presented. Give the groups ten minutes to decide what they, as a group, would like to do better back on the job. (Ten minutes.)

7. List what each group comes up with on a flip chart. (Ten minutes.)

8. Ask the total group to discuss the lessons that can be learned from this activity:

   - How might these new metaphors for your team help you to improve your team's functioning?

   - What might be learned about effective teamwork in general?

   - What have you decided that your team can do differently in the future?

   - How will your team implement these changes? How will you hold yourselves accountable for making the changes?

   (Fifteen minutes.)

Variations

- Have the individual tables/teams/groups create their own lists of potential metaphors.

- Focus specifically on team leadership by using the Teams by Any Other Name Leadership Traits Listing to spark discussion.

Submitted by Robert Alan Black.

Robert Alan Black, Ph.D., CSP, founder and president of Cre8ng People, Places & Possibilities, is a creative thinking consultant and award-winning professional speaker who specializes in the S.P.R.E.A.D.ng™ of Cre8ng™ and Creative Thinking throughout workplaces around the world. Each year he speaks at many executive development institutes, and conferences, conventions in the United States, Canada, Turkey, and South Africa. He has written eleven books and over two hundred articles.

Teams by Any Other Name Metaphors Listing

Instructions: Select three to four nouns from this alphabetical listing that you believe are pertinent for your work team and complete the following statement for each noun: "Our team is like a _____ because _____."

When you have finished, wait until the facilitator gives you further instructions.

a. aquarium

b. bookstore

c. carnival

d. dictionary

e. elephant

f. fan, electric or paper

g. garden

h. harp

i. insect swarm

j. jungle

k. kites and kite flying

l. lunch box

m. mountain range

n. nest

o. orchestra

p. puzzle box

q. quartz, cut

r. river

s. storage building

t. television network

u. umbrella

v. vase

w. weathervane

x. xylophone

y. yacht race

z. zoo

TEAMS BY ANY OTHER NAME LEADERSHIP TRAITS LISTING

Instructions: The following is a listing of terms that have sometimes been used to describe successful leaders. Choose three of the words that you believe are pertinent at this time to describe the type of leader needed by your work team. Jot down some notes after the adjectives you choose so that you can discuss your ideas with your team members when asked to do so.

Adventurous

Boundless energy

Committed

Creative

Curious

Dedicated

Encouraging

Focused

Goal-oriented

Headstrong

Intelligent

Jewels (finds them in people)

Kaleidoscopic, willing to try anything

Loyal

Measures the odds of risk

Negotiates when necessary

Organized for success

Passionate about his or her cause

People-focused

Praises others

Quick to act when necessary

Reduces wasted effort

Secure in his or her thinking

Supportive

Task-focused

Tough

Unwilling to give up

Valiant

Willing to work hard

X-ray vision of problems

Zealous

747. Group Roles:
Determining Their Effectiveness

Goals

- To understand the different kinds of roles played by group members.
- To discover the roles one plays and how the roles are chosen.
- To learn the impact of one's chosen role on other group members.

Group Size

Any number of people who work together as an intact group.

Time Required

Depending on group size, three to four hours is optimal.

Materials

- A copy of the Group Roles Lecturette for the facilitator.
- A copy of the Group Roles Definition Sheet for each participant.
- Flip charts and felt-tipped markers for each subgroup.
- Sheets of colored stickers (three colors needed), preferably round to match the plates, one sheet of each color per subgroup.
- Plastic or paper plates in bright colors.
- A flip chart drawing of the Group Roles Model prepared in advance by the facilitator. (See the Group Roles Definition Sheet.)

Physical Setting

A large enough room for participants to be able to move around while they work.

Process

1. Explain to participants that they will identify and discuss the roles played by various group members. Give the Group Roles Lecturette. (Five minutes.)

2. Break the participants into small groups of people who typically work together. If the entire large group is part of a work process, divide them into smaller groups based on a logical flow or existing task or discussion groups. Five or six participants per group is ideal. Give each subgroup a flip chart and markers.

3. Provide several examples of roles played in groups, such as "peacemaker" or "clown," and have groups brainstorm roles that are played out in their current groups. (Five minutes.)

4. After a few minutes, bring the large group back together to report out. Ask for examples and post the roles they came up with on another flip chart. Combine the lists, noting similar and different roles. Ask the participants what they notice about the roles you have listed on the flip chart. (Ten minutes.)

5. Tell the participants that sometimes it may be helpful to use a model to help frame the roles identified in their current group. Introduce the Dimock Model as a frame of reference by displaying the prepared flip chart and giving everyone copies of the Group Roles Sheet. Explain Dimock's model, going over the various task, maintenance, and nonproductive roles he identified. Discuss with the group where the roles you have listed from their quick brainstorming would fit into the model. (Ten minutes.)

6. Map the flip chart listing by noting a T (task), M (maintenance), or NP (nonproductive) beside each of the roles. Ask again what the group notices about the information depicted, in particular where the majority of the roles played in their work groups fit into the model. (Ten minutes.)

7. Segue into an analysis of the roles each individual plays within the group as determined by themselves and other group members. Say, "Let's do a quick activity called 'What's on Your Plate?'"

8. Distribute three sheets of different colored stickers (one color for task, another for maintenance, and the third for nonproductive roles) and a paper or plastic plate to each person.

9. Note that the roles in Dimock's model are numbered. Ask the participants to determine as specifically as possible the roles they play in their group, number the appropriate colored sticker, and place the stickers (be as specific as possible with the numbers) onto one side of their plate. When they are finished, ask the participants to share what their plates look like with others in their small groups and to discuss with one another whether they would agree or not. (Ten minutes.)

10. Now have each person place stickers on the plates of others in their group (even if those numbers are already present, as seeing several of the same number is confirming) and discuss with other group members the stickers on their plates. (Fifteen minutes.)

11. When the participants have finished placing the stickers onto one another's plates and explaining why, bring them together into the main work group and have each participant share what roles have been placed on his or her plate. Ask for brief comments after each short presentation. (Twenty minutes.)

12. During this discussion, the following are some areas you may wish to focus on:

   - Did any roles show up on your plate that you did not expect?

   - What was the significance of this information for you and how does it impact the group's performance?

   - Did your own assessment of the roles you play in the group match how others see your roles?

   - What was your reaction to receiving stickers from others that you did not agree with?

   (Ten minutes.)

13. Take an inventory of all the roles identified on individuals' plates for the task, maintenance, and nonproductive role categories by a show of hands for each individual role within Dimock's model.

14. Once all individual roles have been identified, inventoried, and mapped onto the model, ask the group what that information reflects about the current state of their group. Reiterate the 30 percent maintenance and 70 percent task optimal role balance. Ask whether their group has the

proper balance and which roles are out of sync, if any. Ask: "Based on the roles mapped, does the group need to make a shift to becoming a more effective group? If so, in what ways and by adding what roles? In particular, emphasize that groups are composed of individuals and so only individuals can make the commitment to the group to make a positive change that moves the overall group forward. (Ten minutes.)

15. Say that you are now going to give them time to make personal commitments to change to ensure that roles played in the group by individuals are productive and effective. These personal commitments to change should be based on the information uncovered on participants' plates, the discussion the small groups had, and understanding of the negative effect that nonproductive roles have on groups.

16. After giving individual members time to determine the personal changes they are willing to make, ask group members to share what they have determined they will be responsible for in shifting this group to a higher plane. (Ten or fifteen minutes.)

17. Close by asking for key learnings from the session and for ideas that could move the entire group forward back in the workplace.

Variation

- To create energy and fun around this activity, have the smaller groups form relays so that only one group member at a time can write a possible group role on the flip chart and that member must pass the baton (marker) onto the next group member.

Resources

Ballew, A.C. (Ed.) (1994). Identifying roles of group members. *Pfeiffer library: Volume 25, theories and models in applied behavioral science.* San Francisco, CA: Jossey-Bass/Pfeiffer.

Dimock, H.G. (1987). *Groups: Leadership and group development.* San Diego, CA: Pfeiffer & Company.

Submitted by Michael B. Dahl, Sara Keenan, and Helene C. Sugarman.

Michael B. Dahl *is currently a human resources consultant at the World Bank Group in Washington, DC, working in the HR team for the Latin American and Caribbean Region. He has a master's degree in economics and business administration, human resources management, from Copenhagen, Denmark. He worked for three years as a human resources officer in the Danish Ministry of Education before entering the World Bank Group in 1999. He recently graduated from the Organization Development Certificate Program at Georgetown University.*

Sara Keenan *is a performance consultant and manager with Booz Allen Hamilton. She recently graduated from the Georgetown University Professional Development Certificate Program in Organization Development. She currently works for Booz Allen's Center for Performance Excellence, supporting the firm's International and Infrastructure Team and facilitating seven different competency-based training programs.*

Helene C. Sugarman *has been an external consultant since 1989 as a principal of Dynamic Communication. Her experience includes twenty years in education, fourteen of them as a theatre teacher for the Prince George's County Board of Education at Suitland High School. She has consulted with small to large companies in the areas of training design and implementation, strategic planning, leadership development, executive coaching and team building. Her master's degree is from Case Western Reserve University. She recently completed the Professional Certificate Program in Organization Development from Georgetown University. She is currently an associate professor, adjunct, at UMUC in business management and organizational development.*

GROUP ROLES LECTURETTE

In today's fast-paced work environment, more and more work is being accomplished in groups or teams. Of course, groups are composed of individuals who tend to play certain roles in these groups based on their previous experience, their personality, and the other people who are in the group, among other criteria. These roles can be described as either task-oriented—doing the work of the group—or maintenance-oriented—helping the group process information. A number of roles that people play can also be described as nonproductive or subverting to the work of a group. People who play such roles need to be identified, and their impact on the group must be minimized to ensure optimal productivity. Some have suggested that the ideal balance between task and maintenance roles in productive groups is 70 percent task and 30 percent maintenance.

We all play different roles, depending on the different groups or teams to which we belong. The roles can vary substantially based on the context of the group or team, the defined hierarchy of the group or team, expectations, levels of expertise, and so on. Sometimes the roles we play are productive and other times these roles are nonproductive.

Today we will identify what roles you play in the group you work with most of the time, shed light on how others view your roles, and try to understand the impact of the various roles on the overall group and the work that is accomplished. After all roles have been identified in each group, we will determine whether or not that group is happy with the status quo or would like to make some changes to become even more effective and productive.

The 2003 Annual: Volume 2, Consulting/© 2003 John Wiley & Sons, Inc.

GROUP ROLES DEFINITION SHEET*

The model that follows is useful for us as group members to gain an understanding of the different kinds of roles being played in all groups, so that you can determine the role(s) you play and how these choices impact the group.

Task Roles

1. Defining problems
2. Seeking information
3. Giving information
4. Seeking opinions
5. Giving opinions
6. Testing feasibility

Group Maintenance Roles

7. Coordinating
8. Mediating/harmonizing
9. Orienting/facilitating
10. Supportive/encouraging
11. Following

Individual Nonproductive Roles

12. Blocking
13. Out of field (of discussion)
14. Digressing
15. Shutting down
16. Checking out
17. Dominating
18. Nay-saying
19. Yes, butting

---

*Source: H.G. Dimock. *Groups: Leadership and Group Development*. San Diego, CA: Pfeiffer & Company, 1987.

748. TRANSITIONS: EXPERIENCING CHANGE IN A SAFE ENVIRONMENT

Goals

- To help participants experience what change feels like in a safe environment.
- To help participants realize the way they personally experience the transition process.
- To become familiar with the nature of change and transitions.
- To help participants interact with people they normally don't have a chance to mix with.

Group Size

Twenty to one hundred people.

Time Required

Fifty minutes.

Materials

- One copy of the Transitions Lecturette for the facilitator.
- A flip chart and felt-tipped markers for the facilitator.
- Four prepared flip charts, each with one of the following questions, prepared in advance:
  - What is changing?
  - What is ending?
  - What will remain the same?
  - What will the new change look like?

- Felt-tipped markers for participants to use while answering the prepared questions.
- Multiples of the four flip charts for larger groups.
- Microphones for larger groups.
- Blank paper and a pencil for each participant.

Physical Setting

A room large enough to accommodate four to twelve tables that can seat five to eight participants each.

Trainer's Note

Although the participants view this activity as an icebreaker or energizer, it is excellent as an introduction to a general discussion about change and transitions or about what needs to be addressed in the workplace around a specific change initiative.

Process

1. Near the beginning of a meeting, conference, or retreat, or when coming back from a break later in the day, ask participants if they are comfortable.

2. Introduce the goals of the activity by saying, "Many people talk about change, but the best way to understand change is to experience it for yourself. Everyone get up and find someone to sit with whom you don't know well or you usually don't have a chance to talk with. Then introduce yourself and talk about some of the changes going on in your respective work areas." (Five minutes.)

3. If people seem to dawdle rather than moving to find partners, remind them, "Rapid response to change is desirable, so please find partners and be seated quickly."

4. Once people are situated and have started to work together for a moment, interrupt and ask them to call out some of the things they were feeling when you first asked them to get up and move, when they were looking for someone to sit and talk with, and after they had a chance to talk for a bit. Record their responses on a flip chart. (Five minutes.)

5. Once you have recorded responses such as "uncomfortable," "skeptical," and "excited," you may want to add some other feelings, such as "anxious," "ambivalent," "confused," and "energized." (Five minutes.)

6. Have them go back to the assigned task for about five minutes. Then pull the total group together and give the Transitions Lecturette. (Ten minutes.)

7. At this point, give each person a marker and have all participants get up and go in turn to each of the four flip charts that were prepared in advance (multiples of four for larger groups) and write their responses to the questions, then return to their original groups. (Five minutes.)

8. Review the responses on each of the flip charts with the group as a whole. Ask how they can use the answers they have come up with to respond to future changes back on the job. (Ten minutes.)

9. Have people discuss the specific changes taking place within their work areas, the transition process, and what their goals/vision of the new change are. Ask them to write notes to themselves about how they will deal with the changes when they return to the job and commit to reinforcing one another during the change process. (Ten minutes.)

Variation

■ Scramble the groups for discussion to gain perspectives different from those in one's own work group.

Submitted by David J. Shevrin and Darlene Van Tiem.

David J. Shevrin, M.P.A., is a founding member of New Perspectives Group, a Michigan-based organization development firm that helps organizations foster healthy and productive work environments. He accomplishes this by helping clients focus on leadership development, needs assessment, strategic planning, change management, and continuous improvement. Mr. Shevrin completed the Planned Change Internship in 1992 and is currently working on a human performance improvement certificate at the University of Michigan-Dearborn.

Darlene Van Tiem, Ph.D., *is an assistant professor and coordinator of the Adult Instruction and Performance Technology program at the University of Michigan-Dearborn. The International Society for Performance Improvement has published two of her books:* Fundamentals of Performance Technology *(2000) and* Performance Improvement Interventions *(2001). Dr. Van Tiem spent twelve years in telecommunications and manufacturing as curriculum manager and training director prior to joining UM-D. She has received three prestigious national awards: ISPI Outstanding Instructional Communicator—2001, ASTD Technical Trainer of the Year—1991, and ASTD Outstanding Leadership in the Automobile Industry—1992.*

TRANSITIONS LECTURETTE

Now that everyone in the room has experienced change in the relatively safe environment of this group, let me ask you a few questions.

Who here felt energized by this activity and enthusiastically looked for someone he or she did not know too well? [Wait for a show of hands.] Great! You are sometimes known as the "early adopters." Congratulations.

Who here hesitated and waited to see what happened before finding a partner? [Again, wait for a response from the group.] That's okay, because most people in organizations tend to behave that way when faced with change.

Finally, who resisted until most people had found partners? [Watch for a response.] That's okay too, because all of us have resisted change at times, especially when we're asked to do something that on the surface sounds silly and has no apparent purpose.

Let me talk briefly about the nature of change and transition and how to help other people manage changes in the workplace. First, "change" is an event or an action that an individual makes in response to some kind of external stimulus, such as a shift in management structure, a new role, a reduction in budget, or implementation of a new program. A "transition" is a feeling or a range of emotions that a person goes through when asked to change. Transition also is a process the organization as a whole and the people in it go through when trying to accommodate a change.

Organizations are getting pretty good at making changes, because in this rapidly changing world there is no other choice. However, organizations are not very good at handling the impact change has on employees, and they often miss the ramifications for the organization in terms of both morale and productivity. During this activity, we will focus on the transition process, what people go through, and how organizations can help employees manage change better.

Everyone experiences change and transitions both in very similar and in very different ways. William Bridges (1980) talks about three phases all people go through when experiencing change in his book, *Transitions: Making Sense of Life's Changes*. He says that all people tend to go through an "ending" or letting go phase, a "neutral zone" or transition phase, and a "new beginning" or an acceptance of a "new reality."

Even though we all tend to go through these same phases during transitions, how we experience them and how we adjust to accommodate changes either at home or at work is unique for each individual. The way a person deals with change and transition is largely based on how that person has dealt with change throughout his or her life, especially those big life-changing events we all are so familiar with.

If you have resisted change your whole life, it should not be surprising to you that you continue to have difficulty accepting it. If you have embraced change in the past, then making changes is probably something that energizes and excites you. Or if you have needed help during times of change in the past, then reassurance and support most likely continue to be important to you.

Everyone experiences change in his or her own unique way and in his or her own time. We all must learn to respect and appreciate our differences and provide a safe and supportive environment for one another. This means helping others to understand the change, why it's important, and how it will help achieve organizational goals.

During each of the three phases of a transition (ending, transition, and new beginning), people tend to go through the full range of emotions: a sense of loss, a sense of uncertainty about what lies ahead, and a mixture of fear, anxiety, and anticipation, just to name a few. It is important that we provide ways for employees to reflect during each phase in the process, both individually and as a group.

During the *endings phase,* it is important for employees to think about what is ending and what is going to remain the same for them personally and for the organization as a whole. For organizations, the programs, policies, and personnel may change, but the culture and the way people treat one another may not.

During the *transition phase* employees need to have some sense of where the organization is going and how they are going to get there. Communication is key. Informing people about what is changing, what activities have to continue (for example, customer service) and what activities can wait (for example, monthly reports) helps them understand what's required of them during the transition. It also sends a message that the organization cares about its employees and wants them to manage the transition successfully.

Once people reach the *new beginning phase,* it is important to recognize and reinforce the new reality. Employees need to know what has in fact changed and what has remained the same. They need to understand the organization's new vision and goals to see how they fit into the new reality and to be clear on what is now expected of them.

Most importantly, everyone needs to feel understood and appreciated throughout the transition process. If all employees feel this way, not only will they manage the change process better themselves, but they will help to create a healthy and productive workplace capable of successfully meeting the challenges of our ever-changing society.

Reference

Bridges, W. (1980). *Transitions: Making sense of life's changes* (pp. 84–88). Reading, MA: Addison-Wesley.

749. THE SKILLED FACILITATOR: WORKING WITH DEEP RESISTANCE*

Goals

- To provide a means for retaining or regaining control of a program when resistance surfaces.
- To bring out issues that may be blocking group process.
- To give a training group the experience of resistance prior to presenting relevant material relating to it.

Group Size

Any number of participants in small groups of five or six people each.

Time Required

Twenty to thirty-five minutes.

Materials

- A flip chart and felt-tipped markers.
- Blank paper and pencils for participants.

Physical Setting

A room large enough to accommodate the small groups working independently. Usually the room in which the training/facilitating is occurring will suffice.

---

*We provide this piece as a service for newer group leaders. It is not, strictly speaking, an experiential learning activity, but we believe it to be a highly useful technique for dealing with group resistance.

Trainer's Note

Every once in a while, even the most accomplished facilitator/trainer will face deep-seated, escalating resistance from a group. This growing resistance may be due to something the facilitator has inadvertently done, or it may be due to something negative having occurred to the group prior to the onset of the program and have nothing whatsoever to do with the facilitator personally or the program itself.

When strong resistance is present, the process starts with the amount of resistance that one might expect at the beginning of any training or team-building program. The problem is that the resistance begins to escalate, regardless of the program content, and begins to be focused on the facilitator. The resistance is almost always aggressive or passive aggressive in nature—and might even reach the point of openly stated mild verbal abuse directed at the program or even at the facilitator personally.

The best strategy is to address the situation as soon as one is aware of it. This might bring the causal factors to the forefront, where the facilitator can address them, work through them, and then continue with the scheduled program. Frequently, however, direct confrontation serves only to produce silence or denial on the part of group members, which results in the resistance increasing. When things reach this state, usually the outcome is a premature close of the program and a very painful experience for everyone involved. There is, however, an alternative process, as outlined below.

Process

1. If you are experiencing resistance from group members, halt the program and explain to the group that you are aware that something seems to be amiss. Give some examples of what you are experiencing, for example, "No one is asking or responding to questions," "People have been walking out and coming back late," or "The few things that have been said strike me as being curt, or even somewhat hostile in tone."

2. Ask the group if something is wrong, or if you have done something that might have produced this effect. If the answer is "yes," find out what happened, respond to it, and continue with the program.

3. If there is no clear answer to your question, give everyone blank paper and a pencil and ask each participant to write down a number that *right now* expresses his or her satisfaction with you and the program up to this point, with "1" being "least satisfied" and "10" being "most satisfied." Inform them that they will not be asked to disclose their answers.

4. Ask the total group to break out into small groups of five or six each and to designate one member to be a spokesperson.

5. Once groups have formed, ask the spokesperson for each group to lead a brainstorming session to "Come up with a list of everything that you do *not* like about the program, about what we have been doing, or about me personally. Please be as specific as you can." (Ten minutes.)

6. After participants have finished, or after ten minutes, ask the spokesperson of the first subgroup to read that group's list out loud. If met with hesitation, warmly assure the group that this is exactly what you want. Maintain good eye contact with the speaker, listen actively, write everything that is said on the flip chart, and thank the speaker when the list is completed. The *only* response you should have is to ask for clarity on an item if you are unsure. Continue until all groups have responded.

7. When the feedback session is complete, repeat the process, but now asking the groups to brainstorm a list of everything that they *do* like about the program, the process, and you personally. (Five minutes.)

8. Repeat the feedback process in exactly the same manner.

9. Respond to any "dislike" item from the first list that requires a response or any action.

10. When this is completed, ask everyone in the room to write down a number that right now expresses his or her satisfaction with you and the program up to this point with "1" being "least satisfied," and "10" being "most satisfied." Again, inform them that they will not be asked to disclose their responses.

11. If you choose, you may ask the total group, "How many experienced a reduction in satisfaction?" "How many experienced an increase in satisfaction?" (The expectation is that there will be no decrease and about a 20 percent increase in satisfaction.)

12. Ask the group if they would like to continue with the program. If the answer is affirmative, take a fifteen-minute break and pick up the program when you get back.

Variations

- This process can be productively used as a training device in dealing with the topics of "resistance" or "change leadership." For it to be effective, the group must have a reasonable amount of experience working with you, for example, at the midpoint or later of a two- or three-day training program or in the middle of a six- to fifteen-week training course.

- The tactic can be sprung on the group with no warning. Once it has been processed, the facilitator can introduce experiential learning through the following activities: "Resistance: A Role Play" (Karp, 1981) followed by an input, "A Positive Approach to Resistance" (Karp, 1988). When the content of the module is complete, go back and process the learnings in the context of the exercise with which you started the module.

References

Karp, H.B. (1981). Resistance: A role play. In *A handbook of structured experiences for human relations training* (Vol. VII). San Francisco, CA: Jossey-Bass/Pfeiffer.

Karp, H.B. (1988). A positive approach to resistance. In J.W. Pfeiffer (Ed.), *The 1988 annual for group facilitators.* San Francisco, CA: Jossey-Bass/Pfeiffer.

Submitted by H.B. Karp.

H.B. Karp, Ph.D., is currently on the faculty of management at Hampton University in Hampton, Virginia. He is also the owner of Personal Growth Systems, a management consulting firm in Chesapeake, Virginia. He consults with a variety of Fortune 500 and government organizations in the areas of leadership development, team building, conflict management, and executive coaching. He specializes in applying Gestalt theory to issues of individual growth and organizational effectiveness. He is the author of many articles and has written or co-authored several books.

750. THE MOTIVATION GRID: UNDERSTANDING WHAT MOTIVATES US

Goals

- To help participants understand what motivates them.
- To learn some principles of motivation.
- To apply motivation principles to real-life situations.

Group Size

From one to six subgroups of four to six members each.

Time Required

One and one-half to two hours.

Materials

- A Motivation Grid Individual Task Sheet for each participant.
- A large Motivation Grid prepared in advance on a flip-chart sheet with twelve rows and three columns.
- A pencil or pen for each participant.
- A flip chart and felt-tipped markers.

Physical Setting

A room large enough to accommodate small groups of four to six people, with movable chairs.

Process

1. Explain that it is always important to understand one's own motivation as well as the motivation of others. Say that during this activity participants will learn something about themselves as well as learn about others.

2. Ask the participants to sit back, relax, and visualize a time when they have been energized and motivated on the job. Tell them to picture the situation in their minds. After a few minutes, tell them to continue visualizing with their eyes closed and silently answer the following questions. Ask the questions in a slow, well-modulated manner.

   ■ What are you doing?

   ■ What sounds do you hear?

   ■ What do you see?

   ■ How do you feel?

   ■ What are you thinking?

   (Ten minutes.)

3. Ask the participants to breathe deeply and to mentally come back to the room. As they are coming back to the present, give everyone a copy of the Motivation Grid Individual Task Sheet and a pencil. Instruct everyone to take ten minutes to fill in the sheet. (Ten minutes.)

4. Form small groups of four to six participants and ask them to share what they have written within their groups. (Five to ten minutes.)

5. When the groups have finished, ask participants in turn to share one word or phrase that summarizes the motivation and energy experienced in the visualization exercise with the large group as you record them on the prepared Motivation Grid at the front of the room. Record only one word per box. If there are additional words, post them at the bottom of the sheet. (Ten minutes.)

6. Reconvene the small groups and ask each team to choose one or two of the words or phrases from the Motivation Grid and do the following two tasks:

   ■ Take five minutes to *create* a single sentence that expresses the principle(s) on the grid about energy and motivation. (*Example:* People are motivated when they feel productive.)

- Within your team, *develop* a three-minute role play or skit that expresses your subgroup's motivation principle.

(Twenty-five minutes.)

7. Call time and have each team share a principle and present its three-minute skit to the group as a whole. (Four minutes per subgroup.)

8. Lead a discussion focusing on the following:
   - What are the key principles of motivation that you discovered today?
   - What is your responsibility as a leader when motivating others?
   - How can you motivate yourself and others when you are not in a leadership role?
   - How can you apply what you learned to real life back on the job?
   - What might you do differently at work as a result of what you learned during this activity?

(Ten minutes.)

9. Wrap up by having people contract to help each other apply their learnings when they return to work.

Variations

- Each group can address several of the principles and eliminate the role play or skit.
- The groups can be asked to judge the presentations. Rewards can be given for the best principles and presentations.

Submitted by Bonnie Jameson.

Bonnie Jameson is a designer, trainer, and facilitator in all areas of human resource development and organization development. She is an associate professor at California State University at Hayward, California, where she designs and teaches courses in the Nonprofit Management Program and the Training for Trainers Certificate Program. Several of Ms. Jameson's experiential learning experiences have been published in previous Annuals. She co-authored Inspiring Fabled Service (Jossey-Bass, 1996) with Betsy Sanders.

THE MOTIVATION GRID INDIVIDUAL TASK SHEET

Instructions

1. Take three minutes to write a summary of your visualization experience below.

   - What were you doing?

   - What did you see?

   - What did you hear?

- What did you feel?

- What did you think?

2. Write down ONE WORD or a SHORT PHRASE that summarizes your visualization experience about energy and motivation. You will be asked to share your word or phrase within your small group.

THE MOTIVATION GRID

751. Read All About It! Writing Vision Statements

Goals

- To discover how others see the organization's or team's vision for the future.
- To reach agreement on the team or organization's vision for the future.
- To learn how to create vision statements.

Group Size

Eight to twenty members of management from the same organization or members of an intact work team.

Time Required

An hour and a half to two hours, depending on group size.

Materials

- Blank paper and pens or pencils for participants.
- A flip chart and felt-tipped markers for each subgroup.

Physical Setting

A room with tables for writing and with movable chairs for breaking into discussion groups.

Process

1. Explain that sometimes an organization or team can go off track simply from having different visions of where they are headed. Say that they will

have the opportunity to work together on the vision and goals of their own organization or team.

2. Break the participants into small groups of three or four participants each and give everyone blank paper and pens or pencils.

3. Have each person, as an individual, write a headline and lead paragraph describing the organization or team in "X" years, including the ways in which it has changed since "today." Tell them to indicate the importance of the each of their ideas to the future of the organization. (Ten minutes.)

4. Now tell the participants to share their "visions" within their small groups and to make a consolidated statement of where the team or organization will be in X years. Give them more paper and a flip chart and markers for recording their final headline and vision and tell them to choose a spokesperson to present it to the total group. Tell them to include everyone's ideas and to be sure that the vision reflects the desires and input from each group member. (Twenty-five minutes.)

5. Bring the entire group together and have each small group spokesperson introduce his or her team members and then read the headline and paragraph representing their vision for the future. (Twenty minutes.)

6. On a flip chart, capture any recurring themes from the groups—what they are seeking in the future. Use the summary to come up with an outline of a vision for the future of the organization or team. (Ten minutes.)

7. Ask whether anyone's ideas were left out and if it is important to include them. If others agree that an idea should be included, find a way to fit it into the vision as it is written on the flip chart. (Fifteen minutes.)

8. Debrief by asking the following questions:

   - What did you learn about the future of your organization as seen by those present today?

   - How satisfied are you with the vision you have created for your team/organization?

   - What do you believe you need to do next to be sure you can live out your vision for the future?

   - Do you feel personally committed to living out the vision as written? Why or why not?

   - What have you learned about writing vision statements?

   (Fifteen minutes.)

9. Give everyone about five minutes to write down some action steps they will take to help the new vision come alive back on the job. (Five minutes.)

10. Ask everyone to share their ideas and create an action plan on the flip chart identifying those who are responsible and a completion date. Say that you will have the results reproduced and distributed to them. (Fifteen minutes.)

11. Wrap up by checking how everyone feels about the future and how committed they are to making it a reality.

———————————

Submitted by Kristin J. Arnold.

Kristin J. Arnold, M.B.A. C.P.C.M., specializes in coaching executives and their leadership, management, and employee teams, particularly in the areas of strategic and business planning, process improvement, decision making, and collaborative problem solving. An accomplished author and editor of several professional articles and books, as well as a featured columnist in The Daily Press, *a Tribune Publishing newspaper, Ms. Arnold is regarded as an expert in team development and process improvement techniques.*

752. Rubber Bands: Envisioning the Future

Goals

- To see the "stretch" involved with accepting change.
- To make visible the pull of the past relative to the pull of the future.
- To use a physical activity to reinforce the learning process.

Group Size

Any group from five to three hundred in an organization undergoing change.

Time Required

Approximately fifty minutes, depending on the length of the discussion.

Materials

- One 1½-inch book ring for each participant and one for the facilitator.
- One large (5 to 7 inches long and ⅝ inch wide) rubber band and one small (3½ inches long and ¼ inch wide) rubber band for each participant. (*Note:* The rubber bands break, so it is important to have extras available.)
- A flip chart and felt-tipped markers.

Process

1. Prior to the activity, insert one each of the small and large rubber bands into metal book rings, one per participant, and close the rings tightly. Keep one ring with rubber bands for yourself.

2. Tell participants that the goal of the activity they are about to do is to help them become more comfortable with the changes taking place in their work setting.

3. Distribute the book rings and rubber bands to participants. *Safety Note:* Caution the participants to check to ensure that the book rings are closed and that both rubber bands are in good shape. Ask the participants to stretch the two rubber bands out from twelve to fifteen inches. Do this with your own rubber bands and book ring. (Actually, you can stretch the rubber bands about eighteen inches, but discourage the participants from using them in this fashion by saying: "These are *not* designed for body-building. When the rubber bands break, and they do, they hurt a lot—it will bring tears to your eyes.")

4. As the participants become comfortable stretching the rubber bands, ask them: "What is happening?" Participants will say that one rubber band stretches more than the other. Ask which one. They will respond with: "The thin one" or "the small one."

5. Draw the participants' attention to your rubber bands and book ring, which should be in the middle as you stretch out the rubber bands. Note that the book ring in the middle represents the participants, but it could also represent their organization. Ask them to think of ways that this metaphor fits their current work situations.

6. Say that one of the rubber bands represents the past and one represents the future. Ask: "Which is stronger for you or your organization—the past or the future? Is the past holding you back or the future pulling you forward?" Lead a brief discussion of their answers and post pertinent comments on a flip chart. (Ten minutes.)

7. For the purpose of managing change, the important thing to note is that the *pull* of the future *must* be stronger than the combined *pull* of the past and the distractions of the present. If not, the organization is probably stuck and will quickly become obsolete.

8. If all participants are from the same company:

   ■ Assign one third of them the task of identifying positive *historical* events that have helped the organization get where it is today (growth, successful product launch, traditions, and so forth). Also have them identify the historical events that may have limited the company in some way (poor hiring decisions, strikes, unsuccessful decision to market a new product or enter a new market, and so forth).

   ■ Assign one third of the participants to the *present*. What is happening right now in the organization? How much of the time and energy is devoted to the *past* (firefighting, fixing the mistakes of the past)? To the *present* (distractions, overload, no financial slack)? To the *future* (laying the foundation for renewal and innovation)? Ask this group to identify examples to support their conclusion.

■ Assign one third of the participants to the *future*. What are the opportunities (pulling them forward)? What are the threats (holding them back)? Which is stronger? What evidence can the group identify to support its position?

(Fifteen minutes.)

9. Bring the groups together and ask them to report on their findings. After all three groups report, ask the combined group if their vision for the future is strong enough to pull the organization into the future. If not, what are they collectively going to do about it? How can they align their intentions for the good of the organization? Post their responses and offer to send everyone copies after the flip chart is transcribed. (Fifteen minutes.)

10. Conclude with what everyone has learned and how they will respond differently now to what is happening in their organization today. (Ten minutes.)

Variations

■ Draw attention to generational differences or to differences in position within the organization, if pertinent. For example, the elderly often spend a lot of their time reminiscing about the past. Visionaries often focus on the future. In contrast, teenagers often devote all of their time to the present, with little appreciation for the efforts of the past or concerns about the future.

■ As a lesson in vision, develop a handout with quotes about the importance of vision and use it as a discussion starter. For example, "When there is no vision, the people perish" (Proverbs 29:18); a vision is a lamppost to illuminate the way; a vision is an act of faith; a vision gives meaning to what we are doing.

Submitted by Bob Shaver.

Bob Shaver, MBA, is a faculty associate and director of the basic management certificate program at the University of Wisconsin-Madison School of Business. He has twenty years of industry and military experience, including ten years in managerial positions as a first-line supervisor, middle manager, and senior manager. For more than ten years, Mr. Shaver has designed and facilitated seminars on the future, instructional skills, leadership, management of change, motivation, problem solving, and survey design.

Introduction
to the Inventories, Questionnaires, and Surveys Section

Inventories, questionnaires, and surveys are valuable tools to the HRD professional. These feedback tools help respondents take an objective look at themselves and their organizations. These tools also help to explain how a particular theory applies to them or to their situations.

Inventories, questionnaires, and surveys are useful in a number of training and consulting situations: privately for self-diagnosis; one-on-one to plan individual development; in a small group to open discussion; in a work team to help the team to focus on its highest priorities; or in an organization to gather data to achieve progress.

You will find that the use of inventories, questionnaires, and surveys enriches, personalizes, and deepens training, development, and intervention designs. Many can be combined with other experiential learning activities or articles in this or other *Annuals* to design an exciting, involving, practical, and well-rounded intervention.

Each instrument includes the background necessary for understanding, presenting, and using it. Interpretive information, scales, and scoring sheets are also provided. In addition, we include the reliability and validity data contributed by the authors. If you wish additional information on any of these instruments, contact the authors directly. You will find their addresses and telephone numbers in the "Contributors" listing near the end of this volume.

Other assessment tools that address a wider variety of topics can be found in our comprehensive *Reference Guide to Handbooks and Annuals*. This guide indexes all the instruments that we have published to date in the *Annuals*. You will find this complete, up-to-date, and easy-to-use resource valuable for locating other instruments, as well as for locating experiential learning activities and articles. A print version of the *Reference Guide* is available for volumes through 1999. An online supplement covering the years through 2003 can be found at www.pfeiffer.com/go/supplement.

The 2003 Annual: Volume 2, Consulting includes three assessment tools in the following categories:

Individual Development

Renewal at Work Self-Assessment, by Krista Kurth and Suzanne Adele Schmidt

Leadership

The Leader Emotional Quotient Survey, by Gerald V. Miller

Organizations

Ten P's: Assessing Corporate Excellence, by Biswajeet Pattanayak, Rajnish Kumar Misra, Phalgu Niranjana, and Sanjyot Pethe

RENEWAL AT WORK SELF-ASSESSMENT

Krista Kurth and Suzanne Adele Schmidt

Abstract: The Renewal at Work Self-Assessment measures four key dimensions of well-being related to balance at work: renewal of the body, mind, spirit, and emotions. The assessment also addresses the individual's general approach to work-life balance. Respondents rate themselves on twenty-four items that describe their attention to the four dimensions throughout their work day and rate themselves on six additional statements related to their overall approach to work-life balance. The results may be used to identify individual development opportunities.

Very few tools assess either renewal at work or balance at work, although numerous articles have been written about work-life balance from both organizational and individual perspectives. Organizations have been encouraged to offer programs such as job sharing, childcare, and elder care and individuals have been challenged to live a more balanced life. Important to the overall concept is the concept of work balance itself. The main questions are (1) Do organizations support renewal and work/life balance? and (2) Do individuals employ renewal strategies throughout the workday to revitalize their bodies, minds, spirits, and emotions?

The Renewal at Work Self-Assessment provides individuals with a tool for assessing their personal approach to and need for renewal at work. The inventory assesses four key areas of renewal: *body, mind, spirit,* and *emotions.* It also addresses the individual's general approach to work-life balance.

The assessment is designed to raise individuals' awareness about their personal approach to balance at work in particular and work-life balance in general. The results may be used to determine the need for making changes in one's approach to work. It is assumed that self-renewal may result in increased perspective, energy, enthusiasm, and creativity. In a group training session, the discussion would most likely address organizational work balance issues.

It is often said that the responsibility for working in a self-renewing way rests with the individual. It may also be said that organizations that are genuinely concerned about their employees' productivity and well-being are advised to support each employee's efforts at self-renewal. Providing employees with opportunities to assess their renewal at work is a good first step in supporting individual self-renewal.

DESCRIPTION OF THE INSTRUMENT

The instrument is composed of thirty questions; twenty-four measure renewal of the body, mind, spirit, and emotions at work. Six measure the individual's general approach to work-life balance.

Participants respond using a four-point scale and can self-score the assessments. Brief interpretative information is included for group discussion.

Theory Behind the Instrument

The instrument is based on the authors' evolving work in the area of proactive renewal at work and on Frederic M. Hudson's (2002) characteristics of self-renewing adults. It includes at least one question related to each of Hudson's ten characteristics. Hudson describes self-renewing adults as follows:

1. They are value-driven.

2. They are connected to the world around them.

3. They require solitude and quiet.

4. They pace themselves.

5. They have contact with nature.

6. They are creative and playful.

7. They adapt to change.

8. They learn from their disappointments and losses.

9. They never stop learning.

10. They are future-oriented.

The assessment takes into account our own ideas about taking responsibility for one's own renewal at work as well as our framework for an integrated model of well-being at work. Our model includes the four key aspects of renewal of one's body, mind, spirit, and emotions. The model also takes into account living a life outside of work that contributes to one's well-being while at work.

Administration of the Instrument

Inform participants that all responses to the survey will be confidential and that any scores revealed to the entire group (if used in a training setting) will represent group averages only. Tell the participants that the survey measures their individual approaches to renewal at work and that the findings will be discussed after the survey has been completed. Give out copies of the self-assessment and pens or pencils. Have people complete the Data Collection

Form if you plan to collect the data for research purposes. If not, respondents may proceed directly to the assessment.

After everyone has completed the assessment, hand out copies of the Scoring and Interpretation Sheet and tell them to tally their scores on the five sections and then compare them with scores in the interpretation grid section by section. Next, ask respondents to complete the remainder of the steps on the Scoring and Interpretation Sheet, noting their own individual levels in the Need for Attention and Change Strategy columns in Step One. Ask everyone to answer the three questions in Step Three honestly and then write any comments that come to mind at the bottom of the sheet. Next, give respondents copies of the Renewal at Work Data Compilation Sheet, have them transfer their numbers to this sheet anonymously, and hand them in to you. Then give everyone a break while you compile the data.

SCORING AND INTERPRETATION

Determine the group's average score for each section. Post these averages on a flip chart, and when everyone has reassembled ask participants to compare the average group scores to their own scores. Lead a discussion of the participants' responses to the findings. Ask if there were any surprises and how participants might make changes that would allow them to practice renewal at work.

If the assessment is being used in a one-on-one coaching setting, simply review the scores with the individual and help the person to identify changes to be made.

The Interpretation Grid on the Scoring and Interpretation Sheet provides participants with the information necessary to understand their own scores. While leading a discussion of the group's scores, ask open-ended questions that promote dialogue. Solicit suggestions for how this information can be used to achieve better balance in the participants' work lives. Ask participants to share strategies that they might employ to renew their own body, mind, spirit, and emotions at work. Give them paper and pencils and ask them to make plans to do so, perhaps with a partner who will serve as a sounding board and a reminder in the future.

Suggested Uses for the Assessment

This assessment may be used to generate dialogue and motivate personal change in one's approach to renewal at work. It may be used in a group training or coaching setting. It is effective with groups from various organizations and intact groups or teams.

Validity

To date, the instrument has not been validated.

Reference

Hudson, F.M. (2002). *Mastering the art of self-renewal: Adulthood as continual revitalization.* New York: Fine Communications.

Krista Kurth, Ph.D., is a co-founder of Renewal Resources, a consulting firm dedicated to the renewal of individuals and organizations. She consults and speaks about, as well as coaches, others on how to lead more renewing and productive lives at work. She and Dr. Suzanne Schmidt have delivered their unique Mastering Personal Renewal at Work program to hundreds of individuals. They are completing their first in a series of books on renewal at work, Running on Plenty at Work: Renewal Strategies for Individuals. Dr. Kurth has held a range of managerial and consulting positions, including one with KPMG Peat Marwick. She received her doctorate in organization development from George Washington University, where she conducted original research on the topic of spiritual renewal in business.

Suzanne Adele Schmidt, Ph.D., is a co-founder of Renewal Resources, a consulting firm dedicated to the renewal of individuals and organizations. She consults and speaks about, as well as coaches, others on how to lead more renewing and productive lives at work. With Dr. Krista Kurth, she has delivered their unique Mastering Personal Renewal at Work program to hundreds of individuals. The two are completing their first in a series of books on renewal at work, Running on Plenty at Work: Renewal Strategies for Individuals. Prior to Renewal Resources, Dr. Schmidt managed human resources for Life Technologies and Westinghouse Electric Corporation. She completed her doctorate at the University of Pittsburgh and co-authored Training Games for Managing Change, published by McGraw-Hill.

RENEWAL AT WORK DATA COLLECTION SHEET

Organization: _____

Department: _____

Gender: Male _____   Female _____

Age (circle one):   20 to 30   31 to 40   41 to 50   51 to 60   61 to 70

Renewal at Work Self-Assessment

Krista Kurth and Suzanne Adele Schmidt

Instructions: For each of the items listed below, circle the number that best indicates how you currently think or feel about yourself at work. There are no "right" or "wrong" answers, only honest descriptions of yourself at work.

Use the following as a key:

1 = Not True of Me   2 = Slightly True of Me   3 = Mostly True of Me   4 = True of Me

Section 1

	Not	Slightly	Mostly	True
1. I am aware of my body's need for a break, food, or physical exercise during the workday.	1	2	3	4
2. I take breaks, eat nutritious lunches, and drink plenty of water during the day.	1	2	3	4
3. My breaks at work include some kind of low-level physical exercise (stretching or walking).	1	2	3	4
4. I pace myself at work, balancing high-energy tasks with time to replenish myself.	1	2	3	4
5. I come to work well-rested.	1	2	3	4
6. I work a reasonable number of hours.	1	2	3	4

Total Score for Section 1 = _____

Section 2

	Not	Slightly	Mostly	True
7. I allow myself to daydream or do breathing exercises during my workday.	1	2	3	4
8. I focus my mind on the present and on the task at hand.	1	2	3	4
9. I look for opportunities to learn and use new skills at work.	1	2	3	4
10. I spend some small portion of each workday in quiet.	1	2	3	4

1 = Not True of Me   **2 = Slightly True of Me**   **3 = Mostly True of Me**   **4 = True of Me**

11. I practice the art of positive self-talk and
     positive imaging while at work.   1   2   3   4

12. I seek openings to be creative and playful
     at work.   1   2   3   4

Total Score for Section 2 = _____

Section 3   Not   Slightly Mostly   True

13. I express my emotions in calm, healthy, and
     appropriate ways at work.   1   2   3   4

14. I sustain work relationships through listening
     and empathizing with others and by doing
     small acts of kindness for others.   1   2   3   4

15. I forgive myself and others for errors and
     learn from disappointments at work.   1   2   3   4

16. I am motivated by and enthusiastic about
     my work.   1   2   3   4

17. I have developed and work by my life
     mission/purpose statement.   1   2   3   4

18. I pay attention to what I am doing or feeling
     and to whether changes are necessary.   1   2   3   4

Total Score for Section 3 = _____

Section 4   Not   Slightly Mostly   True

19. I consider my work a privilege and sacred.   1   2   3   4

20. I take time during my workday to rejuvenate
     myself by connecting with nature in some way.   1   2   3   4

21. I see my work as an opportunity to serve others.   1   2   3   4

22. I look for the larger meaning and purpose in
     situations at work.   1   2   3   4

23. I ask for inner guidance or call on my higher
     power for help during my workday.   1   2   3   4

24. I pray, meditate, or take time for silence
during my workday.   1   2   3   4

Total Score for Section 4 = _____

Section 5

	Not	Slightly	Mostly	True
25. I take all of my vacation days.	1	2	3	4
26. I follow a regular fitness program by exercising at least three times a week for twenty minutes each.	1	2	3	4
27. I have at least one hobby outside of work.	1	2	3	4
28. I spend time with friends and family on a regular basis.	1	2	3	4
29. I am part of a group or community that nourishes my spirit.	1	2	3	4
30. I spend a portion of each week away from work in solitude or in nature.	1	2	3	4

Total Score for Section 5 = _____

Renewal at Work Scoring and Interpretation Sheet

Instructions

Step One: Tally your scores for each section on the assessment itself. Transfer the scores for each section to the Your Score column below.

Section	Your Score	Renewal Quadrant	Need for Attention	Change Strategy
Section 1		Body		
Section 2		Mind		
Section 3		Emotions		
Section 4		Spirit		
Section 5		Work-Life Balance		

Step Two: Compare your scores for *each of the five sections* with the table below to determine how much you need to pay attention to self-renewal at work and the change strategy associated with your score.

Interpretation Grid

Section Score	Need for Attention	Change Strategy
20+	None	None
13–19	Somewhat	Observe
6–12	Probably	Take Action

Write any comments here that will help you find ways to renew yourself while at work.

Step Three: Reflect on all of the above for a few moments. Then answer the following questions as honestly as possible:

1. Did I answer all of the questions honestly?

2. What aspects of my renewal at work require my attention?

3. What would be realistic renewal goals for me to set? Consider the resources (time, people, money) that will help you attain those goals and write them below.

RENEWAL AT WORK DATA COMPILATION SHEET

Section	Your Score	Renewal Quadrant	Need for Attention	Change Strategy
Section 1		Body		
Section 2		Mind		
Section 3		Emotions		
Section 4		Spirit		
Section 5		Work-Life Balance		

THE LEADER EMOTIONAL QUOTIENT SURVEY

Gerald V. Miller

Abstract: Intellect alone, that is, a high IQ (intelligence quotient) is not enough for someone to become an effective leader. Recent research has shown that "brainpower" or intellect is only the beginning. One also has to be emotionally competent. More emotionally competent leaders: are able to recognize, value, and appropriately express their emotions; possess positive self-regard; are capable of understanding and empathizing with the emotions of others; are capable of making and maintaining mutually satisfying personal relationships; are able to be interdependent rather than independent, dependent, and/or co-dependent on others; are able to cope with stress without losing control; are capable of resisting and/or delaying emotional impulses; and lead fairly happy and optimistic lives.

The Leader Emotional Quotient Survey (EQ-s) provides a snapshot of a leader's degree of emotional competency and can be used to identify areas for improvement and to assess his or her progress over time. The leader's EQ profile pinpoints strengths and weaknesses in the leader's overall spectrum of emotional competency. The profile can also be an aid in predicting the individual's ability to succeed on the "human side" of the leadership equation.

The concept of emotional intelligence is rooted in Leeper's work. Leeper (1948) proposed that emotional thought is part and parcel of intelligence in general. He began by addressing the possibility that "emotions as disorganized thoughts" could be the downfall of even a genius. Thirty-five years later, in *Frames of Mind*, Howard Gardner (1983) postulated the concept of "multiple intelligence." Within a category that he named "personal intelligence" (emotional intelligence), he included two components: intra-psychic capacities and interpersonal relationships.

The phrase "emotional intelligence" was coined in 1990 by psychologists Peter Salovery of Yale and John Mayer of the University of New Hampshire. They focused their research efforts directly on the "emotional" aspect of intelligence, primarily categorized into four component areas: emotional self-awareness; stress tolerance; impulse control; and interpersonal relationships.

More recently, in his book, *Emotional Intelligence*, Daniel Goleman (1995) reported on the scientific studies of emotion, showing why and how to bring intelligence to emotions, thus bringing the concept of EQ to the general public. In 1998, in *Working with Emotional Intelligence*, Goleman provided a formula for success at work by classifying emotional competencies into personal competencies, social competencies, and motivation.

The Leader Emotional Quotient Survey (Leader EQ-s) can be used for self-discovery, as a leadership feedback mechanism, for general leadership development, for coaching in the human dimension of leadership, and for many other leadership applications. There are four "cornerstones" or categories of leader EQ: intrapersonal, interpersonal, stress management, and affect, shown in Figure 1 along with their subcategories.

IQ (INTELLIGENCE QUOTIENT) vs. EQ (EMOTIONAL QUOTIENT)

IQ is an index of one's relative level of brightness as compared to others sharing the same chronological age. IQ measures "gi" (general intelligence or cognitive abilities), which is composed of crystallized abilities, fluid/analytic abilities, and short-term memory. Figure 2 outlines this concept.

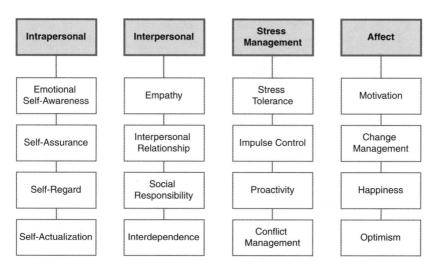

Figure 1.   The Four Cornerstones of Leader EQ-s

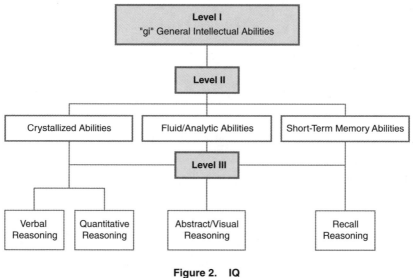

Figure 2.   IQ

EQ, however, is an index of one's relative level of managing and/or coping with psychosocial demands as compared to others sharing the same chronological age. According to Dr. Rueven Bar-On (1996):

> "Emotional intelligence can be defined as an array of capabilities, competencies, and skills which influence one's ability to succeed in coping with environmental demands and directly affect overall psychological well-being."

Goleman emphasizes that emotional intelligence is altered throughout life, lists ways in which basic emotional skills can be improved, and illustrates the price that one pays for what he calls "emotional illiteracy." In his most recent book, *Working with Emotional Intelligence* (1998), he states:

> "The difference between those at high and low ends of the emotional intelligence scale is very large, and being at the top confers a major competitive advantage. Thus 'soft' skills matter even more for success in 'hard' fields." (p. 20)

EQ measures "ge" (general emotional abilities), which is composed of two subsets, emotional knowledge and emotional competency, made up of four components, intrapersonal, interpersonal, stress management, and affect. Figure 3 outlines this concept. Some definitions that are critical for understanding EQ follow.

Definitions

- *Intrapersonal:* The overall ability to examine one's "self" in terms of understanding one's mental modes and self-concept. The intrapersonal components of EQ are

    - *Emotional Self-Awareness:* The ability to recognize one's feelings

    - *Self-Assurance:* The ability to have a strong understanding of one's self-worth and capabilities

    - *Self-Regard:* The ability to respect and accept one's own basic goodness

    - *Self-Actualization:* The ability to realize one's potential capacities, characterized by becoming involved in pursuits that lead to a meaningful, rich, and full life; the ability to be self-directed and self-controlled in one's thinking and actions and to be free of emotional dependency

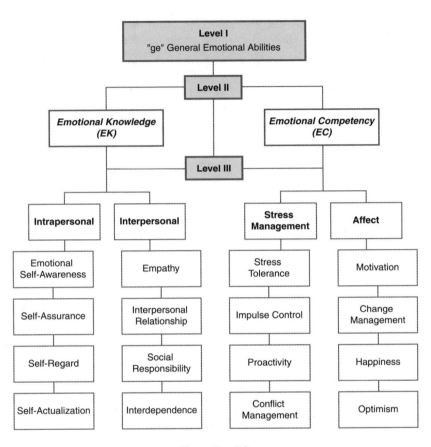

Figure 3.   EQ

- *Interpersonal:* The overall ability to move from the intrapersonal to the interpersonal, in terms of awareness of others and the ability to establish mutually satisfying relationships. The components are

  - *Empathy:* The ability to be aware of, understand, and appreciate the feelings of others

  - *Interpersonal Relationships:* The ability to establish and maintain mutually satisfying relationships that are characterized by intimacy and giving and receiving affection

- *Social Responsibility:* The ability to demonstrate that one is a cooperative, contributing, and constructive member in one's social group

- *Interdependence:* The ability to recognize that in today's "global village" we are mutually dependent on one another and that acting independently will cause harm to oneself and to others

- *Stress Management:* The overall ability to manage one's internal and external responses to the environment. The components of this dimension are

  - *Stress Tolerance:* The ability to withstand, without "falling apart," adverse events and stressful situations

  - *Impulse Control:* The ability to resist or delay an impulse, drive, or temptation to act

  - *Proactivity:* The ability to anticipate and actively deal with an expected difficulty rather than waiting

  - *Conflict Management:* The ability to negotiate and collaboratively resolve differences between what one wants or needs and what another wants or needs

- *Affect:* The overall ability to influence one's psychological state in terms of emotions or feelings, as distinguished from cognition or thought

  - *Motivation:* The ability to set results-oriented goals and take action to achieve those goals

  - *Change Management:* The ability to recognize the need for change, sponsor change, enlist others in and remove barriers to progressive change

  - *Happiness:* The ability to feel satisfied with one's life, to enjoy oneself and others, and to have fun

  - *Optimism:* The ability to look at the brighter side of life and to maintain a positive attitude

BACKGROUND OF THE INSTRUMENT

The EQ surveys developed to date have been cumbersome, time-consuming, lengthy, academic, and therefore, more often than not, irrelevant and impractical for use in the corporate world.

In 1996, Reuven Bar-On developed the first standardized and recognized assessment of emotional intelligence, the Bar-On Emotional Quotient

Inventory, a 133-question assessment. Bar-On provides fifteen content scales grouped into five clusters: intrapersonal, interpersonal, cognition-orientation, stress management, and affect.

Robert Cooper and Ayman Sawaf's 1997 *Executive EQ: Emotional Intelligence in Leadership and Organizations* was the first source to directly relate the concepts of emotional intelligence to the workplace. Cooper and Sawaf provide a four cornerstone approach: emotional literacy, emotional depth, emotional fitness, and emotional alchemy.

With 226 questions, Mayer and Salovery's detailed EQ Map Questionnaire helps one assess his or her emotional intelligence in general or in particular organizational situations. The EQ Map Questionnaire is composed of five sections and eighteen scales.

The works of Goleman, Bar-On, Mayer and Salovery, Cooper and Sawaf, and others demonstrate that the power of emotions is as strong and as effective as the power of the intellect. The Leader EQ-s builds on the foundation of these scholars, but is a more practical application tool.

Constructing the Leader EQ-S

A performance-based approach was taken to developing this instrument. Corporate leaders were asked during leadership training events to do the following:

First: To develop a workable definition of leadership that included both the task side and the human side of the workplace. The following is an aggregate of the responses received:

> Managers handle complexity. Leaders guide and facilitate others to new horizons! Call them the "new" leaders, or—better yet—the new non-administrators or the new non-manager leaders. Obviously, both management and leadership qualities are needed in the workplace. However, the emphasis in business today is on leadership traits.

Based on the responses, leadership competency can be boiled down to four main components of constancy of purpose; congruity of activity; competency of outcome; and compatibility of values (Miller, 1999).

Second: Respondents were also asked to complete the following statements, based on the definition above: (1) An effective leader is one who results in (outcome [a noun]) and (2) An effective leader is one who is (attribute [an adjective]). The survey resulted in the following common keystones:

Emotional Knowledge (EK). When leaders are emotionally knowledgeable, they recognize the purpose and wisdom of emotions. They do not ignore or discount their "feelings" as irrelevant to the tasks of being human or the tasks of being a leader of humans! They possess high levels of emotional self-awareness.

Emotional Competency (EC). When leaders are emotionally competent, they put the skills of emotional consciousness into everyday practice. They are, as the great Buddhist philosophy states, "Be Here Now!" They are authentic and integrated, emotionally as well as intellectually, being fully and emotionally present at any given moment. They practice the EQ skills of emotional self-awareness, empathy, impulse control, and so on, not just "showing up" and "going through the motions" of work relationship duties.

Much has been written about the differences between managers and leaders, and the Leader EQ-s is designed to test for the presence of an awareness of the leadership behaviors and their practice shown in Figure 3.

Of course, awareness (EK) does not automatically equal behavioral change (EC). But awareness must be present before behavioral change can be undertaken. It is for the purposes of raising respondents' awareness of their emotional intelligence that the Leader EQ-s was developed.

THE LEADER EQ-S INSTRUMENT

The Leader EQ-s is designed to assess the emotional quotient and thus the EK and the EC of aspiring, potential, or present leaders on two keystones: emotional knowledge and emotional competency, and four building blocks: intrapersonal, interpersonal, stress management, and affect, with sixteen underpinnings (see Figure 3).

The survey comprises a forty-eight-item self-questionnaire, a questionnaire to obtain feedback from others, a response analysis sheet, an interpretation sheet, and a profile graph on which one can chart results. A sample letter to send to respondents and an action planning outline are also included.

The Leader EQ-s is designed to be completed by the leader him- or herself and by five of the leader's peers, supervisors, or subordinates (the "respondents").

The leader and the respondents are asked to mark whether they strongly agree, are inclined to agree, are inclined to disagree, or strongly disagree with each statement as it applies to the leader. Later, during the analysis and interpretation phase, differences between the leader's self-score and the respondents' are contrasted.

VALIDITY AND RELIABILITY

No reliability data are available on the Leader EQ-s at the present time. The instrument, however, has face validity, as its purpose is to make participants more aware of their emotional quotients through the process of self-analysis and feedback, and it has been shown to accomplish this.

ADMINISTRATION

The following process is suggested for facilitating a workshop on leadership EQ with several participants using the Leader EQ-s.

At least two weeks prior to working with the leader participants, provide each of them with five copies of the Leader EQ-s—Feedback Edition and accompanying Letter to Participants. Tell them to write letters on their own stationery, similar to the sample letter, to respondents. They are to attach their letters to the feedback survey and give them to five peers, supervisors, and/or subordinates who know them well at least a week prior to the date of the workshop. The respondents are to follow the completion instructions and return the surveys anonymously, in a sealed envelope, either to the leader or to you, the facilitator. (*Note:* Be sure to specify on the respondents' letter whether the facilitator is to receive the surveys or whether the leader will be collecting them. The advantages of collecting them yourself are that they are less likely to be forgotten on the day of the workshop and the scoring can be done in advance.) Anonymity allows for more candid responses. If the surveys are returned in time, they may be scored prior to the workshop, but it is important for leaders to do their own interpretation and profiling during the workshop, so as to internalize the results.

SCORING

At the workshop session, before addressing the aggregate results from the leaders' respondents, distribute one copy of the Leader EQ-s-Self to each leader. Instruct the leaders to complete the survey based on their self-assessment of how they are at the present time, not how they might wish to be. Explain that comparisons will be made between their self-assessments and the aggregate feedback from the participants later in the workshop.

The Feedback Edition can be scored either before or during the workshop. Both the Leader EQ-s Response Analysis and the Leader EQ-s Interpretation Sheet sort the forty-eight statements by the four leadership EQ-s building blocks: intrapersonal, interpersonal, stress management, and affect.

Hand out the Leader EQ-s Response Analysis sheets (complete these in advance or ask the leaders to score their own during the session) to the appropriate leader, along with copies of the Leader EQ-s Definitions and the Leader EQ-s Interpretation Sheet. Instruct the leaders to score their own Leader EQ-s-Self results on the Leader EQ-s Response Analysis sheets by putting their answers on the Self blank.

If they are scoring their own Feedback questionnaires, tell the leaders to then transfer their respondents' scores for each question using the following process. They should write in the scores received from each of the five respondents to form a distribution of those scores for each of the items. (Be sure they number the Feedback forms so that data is transferred consistently and profiles can be determined for each respondent.) They should then calculate the average score by adding the others' scores together and dividing by five. Explain this process in detail and do a sample on the flip chart for clarification.

When leaders have finished filling out their Response Analysis sheets, hand out the Leader EQ-s Profile Graph and tell the leaders to plot their totals on the graph. Illustrate this process on the flip chart. Next, refer them to the Leader EQ-s Interpretation Sheets and ask them to analyze their scores. Discuss the meaning of various combinations of scores and have participants share their graphs and relevant thoughts in small groups or in pairs. After everyone has a handle on their results, give out copies of the Leader EQ-s Action Planning Sheet and ask leaders to make action plans to improve their emotional quotient behaviors. Ask everyone to share, as appropriate.

Depending on the size of the group, the scoring, graphing, and interpretation of the Leader EQ-s usually requires thirty minutes to an hour to complete. The discussion phase and action planning will take an additional hour.

Potential Uses of the Instrument

The Leader EQ-s has the following potential uses:

- As part of a leadership training wherein participants have the survey completed by superiors, peers, and/or subordinates prior to the training event. During the leadership training itself, the results can be discussed as the foundation for an EQ workshop.

- As a coaching tool to be administered by a supervisor or a mentor of someone who wishes to improve his or her leadership skills in the EQ arena. The coach can review the results of the Leader EQ-s with the leader and suggest steps for improvement.

- As an assessment tool for future leaders. The results can form the basis of an individual leadership development plan.

- As a process intervention tool for consultants working with leaders. The consultant can show contributions and the value the leaders make to an organization, point out potential pitfalls they have, and give suggestions for improvement and development.

- As a basis for discussion throughout an organization about the relationship between present and desired EQ behaviors and positive leadership styles.

- As a format for any organization that wishes to assess its readiness to implement a more effective style of leadership and an "affective" high EQ organizational culture.

References

Ashkanasy, N.M., Härtel, C.E.J., & Zerbe, W.J. (2000). *Emotions in the workplace: Research, theory and practice.* Westport, CT: Quorum Books.

Bar-On, R. (1996). *The emotional quotient inventory (eq-i): A test of emotional intelligence.* Toronto: Multi-Health Systems.

Boteach, S. (2000). *Kosher emotions: Understand your emotions and master your life.* London: Hodder & Stoughton

Cashman, K. (1998). *Leadership from the inside out: Seven pathways to mastery.* Provo, UT: Executive Excellence.

Chaplin, J.P. (1968). *Dictionary of psychology.* New York: Bantam/Doubleday/Dell

Cooper, R.K., & Sawaf, A. (1997). *Executive EQ: Emotional intelligence in leadership and organizations.* New York: Perigee.

Covey, S.R. (1991). *Principle-centered leadership.* New York: Summit Books.

Fisher, C.D., & Ashkanasy, N.M. (2000). *Emotions in organizations.* Chichester, England: John Wiley & Sons.

Gardner, H. (1983) *Frame of mind.* New York: Basic Books.

Goleman, D. (1995). *Emotional intelligence.* New York: Bantam.

Goleman, D. (1998). *Working with emotional intelligence.* New York: Bantam.

Johnson, R.A. (1986). *Inner work.* New York: Harper & Row.

Leeper, R. (1948). A motional theory of emotions to replace emotions as disorganized responses. *Psychological Review, 55,* 5–21.

Mayer, J.D., & Salovery, P. (1990). Emotional intelligence. *Imagination, Cognition, and Personality, 9.*

Miller, G.V. (1999). The leadership dimensions survey. *The 1999 annual: Volume 1, training.* San Francisco, CA: Jossey-Bass/Pfeiffer.

Peck, M.S. (1978). *The road less traveled.* New York: Simon & Schuster.

Seligman, M.E.P. (1992) *Learned optimism.* New York: Pocket Books.

Singh, D. (2000). *Emotional intelligence at work: A professional guide.* Thousand Oaks, CA: Sage.

Weisinger, H. (1998). *Emotional intelligence at work: The untapped edge for success.* San Francisco, CA: Jossey-Bass.

Gerald V. Miller, Ph.D., is president of Gerald V. Miller Associates, a management consulting and training firm. He consults with a variety of Fortune 500 companies and public organizations in the areas of leadership development and managing change. He has over twenty years' experience as a specialist in management, organization, and human resource development. He blends organizational and leadership assessment and training with productivity improvement strategies so that his customers see a quantitative and qualitative return on their investment.

Leader EQ-s Letter to Participants

To the Leader Participant:

The Leader EQ-s is designed to assess your leadership emotional quotient (EQ) on four dimensions by providing you with feedback about how others view the EQ leadership practices you use.

Attached are five copies of the Leader EQ-s—Feedback Edition. Identify yourself as the person who is being evaluated by writing your name in the blank on each form. Write the date by which you must have the survey returned and whether to return it to you or to the facilitator. Distribute copies of the questionnaire to any five work colleagues (the "respondents"). The respondents should be peers, subordinates, and/or supervisors whom you believe know you well enough to comment on what you would do (and do not do) as a leader. Please distribute all five, as this increases the reliability and validity of the results.

Ask each respondent to complete the questionnaire anonymously and return it to you (or to the facilitator of your EQ leadership workshop) in a sealed envelope. A sample of the letter you can give to respondents explaining the purpose of the Leader EQ-s is shown on the next page.

LEADER EQ-s SAMPLE LETTER TO RESPONDENTS

Dear Respondents:

Attached is one copy of the Leader EQ-s—Feedback Edition. Please fill out the survey about my behavior as a leader to the best of your ability. The purpose of this survey is to assist me in understanding my own behavior as a leader and the impact of that behavior on others in this work setting.

Your honest responses will help me to assess my leadership qualities. Please rate each of my behaviors by following the instructions at the top of the survey.

Do not write your name on the survey form. It is designed to be completed anonymously. Please return the completed survey in a sealed envelope marked to my attention [or to the facilitator].

Thank you for your time and honest feedback.

Sincerely,

[your name]

LEADER EQ-s — FEEDBACK EDITION

Gerald V. Miller

Person being assessed: _____

Date by which to return the survey: _____

Return to whom: _____

Instructions: You have been asked to complete the following survey about the person above. When responding to the statements below, please make choices based on *your perception* of the behavior of the person who requested that you fill out the form. Decide to what extent each of the forty-eight statements applies to this person. For each statement, circle the response that best applies, using the following scale.

Strongly Agree = 3   Inclined to Agree = 2   Inclined to Disagree = 1   Strongly Disagree = 0

This person (the person who asked you to complete this survey about him or her). . .

1. Understands him/herself and holds insights into the reasons for his/her own behavior.	3	2	1	0
2. Is aware of, understands, and appreciates the feelings of others.	3	2	1	0
3. When faced with a dilemma, stops and reflects before acting.	3	2	1	0
4. Has the ability to set high but attainable goals.	3	2	1	0
5. Is self-observant, that is, he/she can internally observe his/her own behaviors, motives, and patterns.	3	2	1	0
6. Is sensitive to the feelings, needs, and sufferings of others.	3	2	1	0
7. Handles stressful situations without becoming anxious.	3	2	1	0
8. Can be described as a "can do" person.	3	2	1	0

9. Accepts his/her strengths and weaknesses as part of who he/she is.	3	2	1	0
10. Really cares what happens to others and is able to feel empathy for them.	3	2	1	0
11. Views problem situations as "challenges," not as obstacles.	3	2	1	0
12. Is a highly motivated individual.	3	2	1	0
13. Openly expresses thoughts, beliefs, and feelings in a nondestructive manner.	3	2	1	0
14. Has close relationships that are characterized by intimacy and the giving and receiving of affection.	3	2	1	0
15. Has the ability to resist or delay an impulse or drive.	3	2	1	0
16. Is flexible when responding to change.	3	2	1	0
17. Is considered to be free of emotional dependency.	3	2	1	0
18. Has friendships that mean a great deal to him/her and to his/her friends.	3	2	1	0
19. Can resist temptation to act on an impulse.	3	2	1	0
20. Can smoothly manage the demands of a changing environment.	3	2	1	0
21. Is self-directed and self-controlled in thoughts and actions.	3	2	1	0
22. Can establish and maintain mutually satisfying relationships.	3	2	1	0
23. Can keep destructive emotions and impulses in check.	3	2	1	0
24. Is willing to make sacrifices to further a needed change.	3	2	1	0
25. Respects and accepts him/herself as basically being a good person.	3	2	1	0

Strongly Agree = 3	Inclined to Agree = 2	Inclined to Disagree = 1	Strongly Disagree = 0

26. Believes that we are all our "brothers' keepers."	3	2	1	0
27. Can be described as a person ready to seize opportunities.	3	2	1	0
28. Has the ability to feel satisfied with his/her life.	3	2	1	0
29. Has good self-regard and self-respect.	3	2	1	0
30. Would never take advantage of someone, even if that person deserved it.	3	2	1	0
31. Can cut through or go around red tape, when necessary, to achieve desired results.	3	2	1	0
32. Gets enjoyment from being alive.	3	2	1	0
33. Has the ability to assess his/her personal strengths and weaknesses realistically.	3	2	1	0
34. Is a cooperative, contributing, and constructive member of society.	3	2	1	0
35. Anticipates and prepares for events rather than reacting to situations.	3	2	1	0
36. Has the ability to enjoy him/herself and others and to have fun.	3	2	1	0
37. Can focus on the development of his/her individual and unique potential and abilities.	3	2	1	0
38. Has the ability to realize that he/she operates in an interdependent world rather than acts independently.	3	2	1	0
39. Can disagree reasonably without attacking others in conflict situations.	3	2	1	0
40. Is optimistic about most things in life.	3	2	1	0
41. Is involved in pursuits that lead to a meaningful, rich, full life.	3	2	1	0
42. Can be described as a cooperative and collaborative person.	3	2	1	0

43. Can listen to differences of opinion with
    an open mind.   3   2   1   0

44. Can maintain a positive attitude, even in
    the face of adversity.   3   2   1   0

45. Tries to make his/her life as meaningful and
    purposeful as possible.   3   2   1   0

46. Works toward mutual, collaborative teamwork
    and consensus.   3   2   1   0

47. Seeks solutions that will be a "win-win" for all
    concerned.   3   2   1   0

48. Has the ability to look at the brighter side
    of life.   3   2   1   0

LEADER EQ-s — SELF

Gerald V. Miller

Name: _____

Date: _____

Introduction

The Leader EQ-s Self provides the opportunity for you to construct a summary of your own perceptions of your EQ-s by indicating the extent to which you agree that each statement accurately describes the way you think, feel, or act in the capacity of a leader, most of the time and in most situations.

There are no "right" or "wrong" answers and no "good" or "bad" choices; the rating that best describes you is the correct answer! Answer openly and honestly by indicating how you actually are, not how you would like to be or how you would like others to think of you.

Instructions

Read each of the forty-eight statements below and decide to what extent it applies to you. For each statement, circle the response that best applies, using the following scale.

Strongly Agree = 3   **Inclined to Agree = 2**   **Inclined to Disagree = 1**   **Strongly Disagree = 0**

1. I understand myself and hold insights into the reasons for my own behavior.	3	2	1	0
2. I am aware of, understand, and appreciate the feelings of others.	3	2	1	0
3. When I am faced with a dilemma, I stop and reflect before acting.	3	2	1	0
4. I have the ability to set high but attainable goals.	3	2	1	0
5. I am able to self-observe, that is, I can internally observe my own behaviors, motives, and patterns.	3	2	1	0
6. I am sensitive to the feelings, needs, and sufferings of others.	3	2	1	0

7. In general, I handle stressful situations without becoming anxious.   3   2   1   0

8. I would describe myself as a "can do" person.   3   2   1   0

9. I accept my strengths and weaknesses as part of who I am.   3   2   1   0

10. I really care what happens to others and am able to feel empathy for them.   3   2   1   0

11. I view problem situations as "challenges," not as obstacles.   3   2   1   0

12. I am a highly motivated individual.   3   2   1   0

13. I openly express thoughts, beliefs, and feelings in a nondestructive manner.   3   2   1   0

14. My close relationships are characterized by intimacy and the giving and receiving of affection.   3   2   1   0

15. I have the ability to resist or delay an impulse or drive.   3   2   1   0

16. I am flexible when responding to change.   3   2   1   0

17. I consider myself to be free of emotional dependency.   3   2   1   0

18. My friendships mean a great deal to me and to my friends.   3   2   1   0

19. I can resist the temptation to act on an impulse.   3   2   1   0

20. I smoothly manage the demands of a changing environment.   3   2   1   0

21. I am self-directed and self-controlled in my thoughts and actions.   3   2   1   0

22. I establish and maintain mutually satisfying relationships.   3   2   1   0

23. It is easy for me to keep destructive emotions and impulses in check.   3   2   1   0

Strongly Agree = 3   Inclined to Agree = 2   Inclined to Disagree = 1   Strongly Disagree = 0

24. I am willing to make sacrifices to further a
    needed change.   3   2   1   0

25. I respect and accept myself as basically being
    a good person.   3   2   1   0

26. I believe we are all our "brothers' keepers."   3   2   1   0

27. I would describe myself as a person ready to
    seize opportunities.   3   2   1   0

28. I have the ability to feel satisfied with my life.   3   2   1   0

29. I have good self-regard and self-respect.   3   2   1   0

30. I would never take advantage of someone,
    even it the person deserved it.   3   2   1   0

31. I will cut through or go around red tape, when
    necessary, to achieve desired results.   3   2   1   0

32. I get enjoyment from being alive.   3   2   1   0

33. I have the ability to assess my personal strengths
    and weaknesses realistically.   3   2   1   0

34. I am a cooperative, contributing, and construc-
    tive member of society.   3   2   1   0

35. I anticipate and prepare for events rather
    than react to situations.   3   2   1   0

36. I have the ability to enjoy myself and others
    and to have fun.   3   2   1   0

37. I focus on the development of my individual
    and unique potential and abilities.   3   2   1   0

38. I have the ability to realize that I operate in
    an interdependent world rather than act
    independently.   3   2   1   0

39. In conflict situations, I can disagree reasonably
    without attacking others.   3   2   1   0

40. I am optimistic about most things in life.   3   2   1   0

41. I am involved in pursuits that lead to a
    meaningful, rich, and full life.   3   2   1   0

42. I would describe myself as a cooperative and collaborative person.	3	2	1	0
43. I listen to differences of opinion with an open mind.	3	2	1	0
44. I can maintain a positive attitude, even in the face of adversity.	3	2	1	0
45. I try to make my life as meaningful and purposeful as possible.	3	2	1	0
46. I work toward mutual, collaborative teamwork and consensus.	3	2	1	0
47. I seek solutions that will be a "win-win" for all concerned.	3	2	1	0
48. I have the ability to look at the brighter side of life.	3	2	1	0

LEADER EQ-S RESPONSE ANALYSIS

Instructions: First, number the feedback sheets you received from respondents and then transfer the numerical answers for each question to the appropriate spot below. Please place each respondent's answer below the number that represents him or her (1 through 5). Then compute an average respondent score and place it on the appropriate blank and place your own score for that item on the Self blank.

Intrapersonal

Self-Awareness

1. I understand myself and hold insights into the reasons for my own behavior.

    Self: _____

    Average of Others: _____

    Others' Distribution:

1	2	3	4	5

5. I am able to self-observe, that is, I can internally observe my own behaviors, motives, and patterns.

    Self: _____

    Average of Others: _____

    Others' Distribution:

1	2	3	4	5

9. I accept my strengths and weaknesses as part of who I am.

    Self: _____

    Average of Others: _____

    Others' Distribution:

1	2	3	4	5

Self-Assurance

13. I openly express thoughts, beliefs, and feelings in a nondestructive manner.

    Self: _____

    Average of Others: _____

    Others' Distribution:

1	2	3	4	5

17. I consider myself to be free of emotional dependency.

    Self: _____

    Average of Others: _____

    Others' Distribution:

1	2	3	4	5

21. I am self-directed and self-controlled in my thoughts and actions.

    Self: _____

    Average of Others: _____

    Others' Distribution:

1	2	3	4	5

Self-Regard

25. I respect and accept myself as basically being a good person.

    Self: _____

    Average of Others: _____

    Others' Distribution:

1	2	3	4	5

29. I have good self-regard and self-respect.

    Self: _____

    Average of Others: _____

    Others' Distribution:

1	2	3	4	5

33. I have the ability to assess my personal strengths and weaknesses realistically.

Self: _____

Average of Others: _____

Others' Distribution:

1	2	3	4	5

Self-Actualization

37. I focus on the development of my individual and unique potential and abilities.

Self: _____

Average of Others: _____

Others' Distribution:

1	2	3	4	5

41. I am involved in pursuits that lead to a meaningful, rich, and full life.

Self: _____

Average of Others: _____

Others' Distribution:

1	2	3	4	5

45. I try to make my life as meaningful and purposeful as possible.

Self: _____

Average of Others: _____

Others' Distribution:

1	2	3	4	5

Totals for Intrapersonal

Compute the average for self and other ratings here and in each instance below by adding the scores and dividing by the number of items answered in each category.

Self: _____   Others: _____

Interpersonal

Empathy

2. I am aware of, understand, and appreciate the feelings of others.

   Self: _____

   Average of Others: _____

   Others' Distribution:

1	2	3	4	5

6. I am sensitive to the feelings, needs, and sufferings of others.

   Self: _____

   Average of Others: _____

   Others' Distribution:

1	2	3	4	5

10. I really care what happens to others and am able to feel empathy for others.

    Self: _____

    Average of Others: _____

    Others' Distribution:

1	2	3	4	5

Relationships

14. My close relationships are characterized by intimacy and the giving and receiving of affection.

    Self: _____

    Average of Others: _____

    Others' Distribution:

1	2	3	4	5

18. My friendships mean a great deal to me and to my friends.

Self: _____

Average of Others: _____

Others' Distribution:

1	2	3	4	5

22. I establish and maintain mutually satisfying relationships.

Self: _____

Average of Others: _____

Others' Distribution:

1	2	3	4	5

Social Responsibility

26. I believe we are all our "brothers' keepers."

Self: _____

Average of Others: _____

Others' Distribution:

1	2	3	4	5

30. I would never take advantage of someone, even if the person deserved it.

Self: _____

Average of Others: _____

Others' Distribution:

1	2	3	4	5

34. I am a cooperative, contributing, and constructive member of society.

Self: _____

Average of Others: _____

Others' Distribution:

1	2	3	4	5

Interdependence

38. I have the ability to realize that I operate in an interdependent world rather than act independently.

Self: _____

Average of Others: _____

Others' Distribution:

1	2	3	4	5

42. I would describe myself as a cooperative and collaborative person.

Self: _____

Average of Others: _____

Others' Distribution:

1	2	3	4	5

46. I work toward mutual, collaborative teamwork and consensus.

Self: _____

Average of Others: _____

Others' Distribution:

1	2	3	4	5

Totals for Interpersonal

Self: _____   Others: _____

Stress Management

Stress Tolerance

3. When I am faced with a dilemma, I stop and reflect before acting.

Self: _____

Average of Others: _____

Others' Distribution:

1	2	3	4	5

7. In general, I handle stressful situations without becoming anxious.

Self: _____

Average of Others: _____

Others' Distribution:

1	2	3	4	5

11. I view problem situations as "challenges," not as obstacles.

Self: _____

Average of Others: _____

Others' Distribution:

1	2	3	4	5

Impulse Control

15. I have the ability to resist or delay an impulse or drive.

Self: _____

Average of Others: _____

Others' Distribution:

1	2	3	4	5

19. I can resist the temptation to act on an impulse.

Self: _____

Average of Others: _____

Others' Distribution:

1	2	3	4	5

23. It is easy for me to keep destructive emotions and impulses in check.

Self: _____

Average of Others: _____

Others' Distribution:

1	2	3	4	5

Proactivity

27. I would describe myself as a person ready to seize opportunities.

    Self: _____

    Average of Others: _____

    Others' Distribution:

1	2	3	4	5

31. I will cut through or go around red tape, when necessary, to achieve desired results.

    Self: _____

    Average of Others: _____

    Others' Distribution:

1	2	3	4	5

35. I anticipate and prepare for events rather than react to situations.

    Self: _____

    Average of Others: _____

    Others' Distribution:

1	2	3	4	5

Conflict Management

39. In conflict situations, I can disagree reasonably without attacking others.

    Self: _____

    Average of Others: _____

    Others' Distribution:

1	2	3	4	5

43. I listen to differences of opinion with an open mind.

    Self: _____

    Average of Others: _____

    Others' Distribution:

1	2	3	4	5

47. I seek solutions that will be a "win-win" for all concerned.

Self: _____

Average of Others: _____

Others' Distribution:

1	2	3	4	5

Totals for Stress Management

Self: _____   Others: _____

Affect

Motivation

4. I have the ability to set high but achievable goals.

Self: _____

Average of Others: _____

Others' Distribution:

1	2	3	4	5

8. I would describe myself as a "can do" person.

Self: _____

Average of Others: _____

Others' Distribution:

1	2	3	4	5

12. I am a highly motivated individual.

Self: _____

Average of Others: _____

Others' Distribution:

1	2	3	4	5

Change Management

16. I am flexible when responding to change.

    Self: _____

    Average of Others: _____

    Others' Distribution:

1	2	3	4	5

20. I smoothly manage the demands of a changing environment.

    Self: _____

    Average of Others: _____

    Others' Distribution:

1	2	3	4	5

24. I am willing to make sacrifices to further a needed change.

    Self: _____

    Average of Others: _____

    Others' Distribution:

1	2	3	4	5

Happiness

28. I have the ability to feel satisfied with my life.

    Self: _____

    Average of Others: _____

    Others' Distribution:

1	2	3	4	5

32. I get enjoyment from being alive.

    Self: _____

    Average of Others: _____

    Others' Distribution:

1	2	3	4	5

36. I have the ability to enjoy myself and others and to have fun.

Self: _____

Average of Others: _____

Others' Distribution:

1	2	3	4	5

Optimism

40. I am optimistic about most things in life.

Self: _____

Average of Others: _____

Others' Distribution:

1	2	3	4	5

44. I can maintain a positive attitude, even in the face of adversity.

Self: _____

Average of Others: _____

Others' Distribution:

1	2	3	4	5

48. I have the ability to look at the brighter side of life.

Self: _____

Average of Others: _____

Others' Distribution:

1	2	3	4	5

Totals for Affect

Self: _____   Others: _____

LEADER EQ-S DEFINITIONS

- *Intrapersonal:* The overall ability to examine one's "self" in terms of understanding one's mental modes and self-concept. The intrapersonal components of EQ are

    - *Emotional Self-Awareness:* The ability to recognize one's feelings

    - *Self-Assurance:* The ability to have a strong understanding of one's self-worth and capabilities

    - *Self-Regard:* The ability to respect and accept one's own basic goodness

    - *Self-Actualization:* The ability to realize one's potential capacities, characterized by becoming involved in pursuits that lead to a meaningful, rich, and full life; the ability to be self-directed and self-controlled in one's thinking and actions and to be free of emotional dependency

- *Interpersonal:* The overall ability to move from the intrapersonal to the interpersonal, in terms of awareness of others and the ability to establish mutually satisfying relationships. The components are

    - *Empathy:* The ability to be aware of, understand, and appreciate the feelings of others

    - *Interpersonal Relationships:* The ability to establish and maintain mutually satisfying relationships that are characterized by intimacy and giving and receiving affection

    - *Social Responsibility:* The ability to demonstrate that one is a cooperative, contributing, and constructive member in one's social group

    - *Interdependence:* The ability to recognize that in today's "global village" we are mutually dependent on one another and that acting independently will cause harm to oneself and to others

- *Stress Management:* The overall ability to manage one's internal and external responses to the environment. The components of this dimension are

    - *Stress Tolerance:* The ability to withstand, without "falling apart," adverse events and stressful situations

    - *Impulse Control:* The ability to resist or delay an impulse, drive, or temptation to act

    - *Proactivity:* The ability to anticipate and actively deal with an expected difficulty rather than waiting

- *Conflict Management:* The ability to negotiate and collaboratively resolve differences between what one wants or needs and what another wants or needs
- *Affect:* The overall ability to influence one's psychological state in terms of emotions or feelings, as distinguished from cognition or thought
  - *Motivation:* The ability to set results-oriented goals and take action to achieve those goals
  - *Change Management:* The ability to recognize the need for change, sponsor change, enlist others in and remove barriers to progressive change
  - *Happiness:* The ability to feel satisfied with one's life, to enjoy oneself and others, and to have fun
  - *Optimism:* The ability to look at the brighter side of life and to maintain a positive attitude

LEADER EQ-S INTERPRETATION SHEET

Instructions: The most crucial step in the learning process is to answer the questions: "So what?" and "Now what?" Now that you have completed your Leader EQ-s Response Analysis sheet, you can interpret the scores and take action to improve your EQ leadership practices. Utilizing what you have learned about how you behave in real work-world leadership situations, you can make plans for your individual professional development.

The Leader EQ-s is best interpreted on an item-by-item basis, as well as by comparison of total category scores. You will be able to determine the following information from your scores.

Individual Item Scores

Average scores of respondents for individual items of 2.0 and above reflect strengths, that is, respondents are stating that they observe your use of this practice.

Average scores of 1.7 to 1.9 are questionable, that is, the total itself provides insufficient information on which to draw a conclusion. You must instead look at the spread of the five scores to determine whether the average score reflects a strength or a weakness. For example, you may receive a score of 1.8 because four respondents were "inclined to agree" about that item and one person rated it "inclined to disagree." This would not necessarily reflect a weakness rating from the majority. However, if you received one "strongly agree," one "inclined to agree" and two "inclined to disagree," you need to improve on that item.

Average scores of 1.6 or below reflect a weakness.

Category Scores

For each dimension, look at the average total score (sum of all the scores averaged by number of items in that category). Use the following scale to determine your skill level:

Scores	Interpretation
24.5 to 36	Excellent employment of the skills
12.5 to 24	Skills are adequate, but could be improved
0 to 12	Skills need significant improvement

This will help you to apply what you have learned about yourself. For best results, focus on dimensions on which you scored between 12.5 and 24 (areas for improvement) and between 0 and 12 (areas requiring concerted effort).

Also, address the individual questions on which your average score was 1.6 or lower, reflecting a weakness, and between 1.7 and 1.9, reflecting a "wait and see" attitude on the part of the respondents.

What can you do to make improvements in each of the categories? Read all of the suggestions that follow the interpretation of your scores and then complete the Leader EQ-s Action Planning Sheet.

Objectivity Scores

Discrepancies of greater than 1.1, in either direction, between your predicted score for an item on the Leader EQ-s—Self and your average feedback score on the Leader EQ-s—Feedback Edition reflect a weakness in objectivity. That is to say, others hold a different view of your EQ knowledge and competency than you do. This can often be a rude awakening. You need to work harder on being the kind of person you believe yourself to be.

If your own score is substantially lower than the feedback you received, it may reflect the fact that you genuinely believe you are ineffective at that practice. You might be prone to change this practice when, in fact, your people are saying that you practice the skill effectively. The opposite holds true. If your score is substantially higher than the average feedback, it may reflect that you genuinely believe that you are effective at that practice. You might be prone to continue a behavior when in fact your people are saying that you need to stop or change that behavior.

Keystone Improvements

What can you do to make improvements in each of the EQ building blocks? Read all of the suggestions that follow the interpretation of your scores and then complete the Action Planning Sheet.

Intrapersonal

A score of 0 to 12 indicates the following areas require improvement:

- *Emotional Self-Awareness:* Better recognition and acceptance of emotions and the role they play, hand-in-glove, with intellect (cognitive abilities).

- *Self-Assurance:* Augment candid sense of your personal self-worth and capabilities.

- *Self-Regard:* Increase courage that comes from accepting yourself as basically good and decent.

- *Self-Actualization:* Accelerate focus on what is personally fulfilling.

Suggestions for Improvement

- Seek out a mentor or counselor who can objectively help you determine what emotions you are feeling and when.

- Visualize often that you are being applauded by a large audience of your peers, similar to the Academy Awards, and practice saying "thank you" without doubting or explaining.

- Keep an "emotional reactions journal" identifying the links between *antecedent* (cause of emotion), *behavior* (how the emotion was expressed), and *consequences* (affect on self, others, and performance).

- Take an experiential, personal growth workshop focused on emotional awareness and actualization.

Interpersonal

Scores of 0 to 12 indicate the following areas need improvement:

- *Empathy:* Increase sense of others' feelings and a dynamic interest in others' needs and concerns.

- *Interpersonal Relations:* Cultivate relationships that are intrinsic and mutually giving.

- *Social Responsibility:* Increase involvement with others in altruistic activities that move society forward.

- *Interdependence:* Increase understanding of the destructiveness of independent behavior in an interdependent world.

Suggestions for Improvement

- Place yourself in circumstances that are way beyond your norm, that is, in someone else's shoes. For instance, if you are not "handicapped," try mailing an envelope while in a wheelchair.

- Keep an "interpersonal rating journal" containing psychological and emotional exceptions of you and the other(s); areas where you need to show sensitivity as requested by the other(s); and development of a feedback loop wherein you receive measurable, observable behavioral improvement indicators from the other(s).

- Volunteer for social service activities that are well beyond your norm, such as AIDS patient assistance.

- Take an experiential workshop focused on interdependent communications and cooperation as the only method to problem solve a dilemma, such as a survival activity.

Stress Management

Scores of 0 to 12 indicate the following areas need improvement:

- *Stress Tolerance:* Appreciate the distinctions between "event" and "ongoing" stressors and develop a "this too will pass" attitude.

- *Impulse Control:* Increase control over destructive emotions and impulses.

- *Proactivity:* Adopt an attitude of "planned future" by looking for patterns and adjusting to events before they happen.

- *Conflict Management:* Avoid confrontation and compromise as resolution strategies; learn to believe in and practice collaboration (win-win) as a viable strategy.

Suggestions for Improvement

- With the aid of a mentor or counselor, place yourself in a stressful situation and practice "counter-conditioning," such as the following methods:
  - Systematic desensitization, the pairing of relaxation with hierarchically arranged anxiety-evoking events
  - Relaxation training
  - Constructing anxiety hierarchies
  - Desensitization in imagination or in reality
- Keep an "impulse control journal" that links antecedent (emotional triggers); behavior (reaction to the emotion); consequence (negative affect on self or others and on performance).

- Make a corrective plan that lists internal response (self-talk) and external behavior (measurable, observable action to correct the situation).

- Take an experiential workshop focused on creativity and innovation that forces you to go outside your traditional realm, such as visioning and transforming work.

- Practice "dialogue" rather than discussion in conflict situations (dialogue operates similar to Windows on your computer; put your ideas on the side, minimize them, and actively listen before responding).

Affect

Scores of 0 to 12 indicate the following areas need improvement:

- *Motivation:* Adopt a "can do" attitude that emphasizes the "benefits" you desire rather than the "features" of any activity.

- *Change Management:* Embrace the attitude that change is positive and enriching.

- *Happiness:* Increase your ability to feel content with your personal and professional life.

- *Optimism:* Accelerate your ability to find the positive side of life.

Suggestions for Improvement

- Keep a "motivation journal."
    - List the "benefits," the motivators, and what would make you want to be the best at what you do
    - Indicate where and how you can acquire the above benefits
    - Cite how you or others are to reward you with the benefits
- Incorporate into your thinking process the following mantra: "The only thing permanent is change!"
- Volunteer for a change project so that you can immerse yourself in managing change in today's changing environment
- Develop a "happiness scale" like the following to rate the activities of your day:

    Enriching = 3   Satisfying =2   Nominal =1   Disappointing = 0

Rule of Thumb: For every five items listed, your "happiness scale" should be between 10 and 15.

- For items rated nominal (1) and disappointing (0), develop an action plan to eliminate or moderate that item.

- Develop an A-B-C (adversity-belief-consequence) record. Over a week, record five A-B-C sequences from your life, listing what the adversity was, your belief about it, and the consequence. After you have recorded five, read them over carefully, looking for the links between your beliefs and the consequences. (*Hint:* You will probably find that pessimistic thinking sets off feelings of inadequacy and rejection, whereas any optimistic thinking sets off feelings of achievement and problem solving.)

- Change all pessimistic "rumination" verbiage (can't, never, won't, and so on) into positive "causation" verbiage (I will, I am going to, It is possible, and so forth). On a daily basis practice eliminating the pessimistic thinking by changing rumination to causation verbiage.

LEADER EQ-S PROFILE GRAPH

Instructions: Plot your own profile for the Leader EQ-s on the graph below, based on your total scores from the Response Analysis.

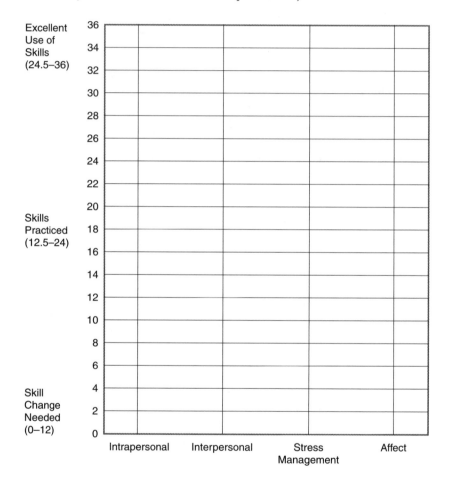

LEADER EQ-S ACTION PLANNING SHEET

Diagnosis

The EQ area in which I scored the lowest was: _____

List the statements on which your average other score was 1.6 or lower. These indicate areas for improvement.

List any statements in the other three EQ areas for which you scored 1.6 or lower.

Based on the above list of statements and your experience with the Leader EQ-s in general, fill in the following information.

My major EQ areas of strength are:

EQ behaviors I do that account for these strengths are:

My major EQ areas for improvement (weaknesses) are:

The behaviors I do or do not do that account for these weaknesses are:

Planning

In order to improve my Emotional Quotient I must:

Continue doing:

Start doing:

Stop doing:

My sources for help include:

Possible mentors:

Available training:

Readings and resources:

Other:

To ensure success I will:

I will know I have been successful when:

I will improve by taking the following specific action steps:

Action Steps	Start Date	Date Completed

TEN P's: ASSESSING CORPORATE EXCELLENCE

Biswajeet Pattanayak, Rajnish Kumar Misra,
Phalgu Niranjana, and Sanjyot Pethe

Abstract: In today's competitive business environment, corporate excellence is no longer a long-term
goal, but an imperative. The term corporate excellence itself is used everywhere, yet it lacks definition
as well as a way to measure it. A tool for understanding the attributes of corporate excellence and hence
predicting when corporate excellence will be present is given here.

A growing body of research demonstrates that such traditional performance measures as return on assets, and even the more contemporary economic profit calculations, are poor gauges of future organizational performance (Kaplan & Norton, 1992, 1996). Of the twenty-five best-performing company stocks for 1990, based on one-year total shareholder return, for example, only one was still among the top twenty-five performers by 1999. Of the thirty-six companies profiled in the 1986 best seller *In Search of Excellence* (Peters, 1988), three are no longer listed on a stock exchange and only twelve outperformed the Standard & Poors 500 Index over the past five years. Clearly, we need better ways to measure present results and momentum. Since excellent performance can be defined either on the basis of reputation or through objective analysis, a model that integrates both dimensions enables us to identify "the best of the best" in the new millennium (Schmidt, 1999).

In order to excel, corporations need to anticipate what the requirements of the 21st Century will be. A myriad of predictions of attributes needed for future success is provided in the literature. For example, it is said that many of the functions now handled in-house will have to be performed through alliances, joint ventures, and networks. It has also been predicted that shifting portfolios of businesses and assets and continuously evolving external networks will make organizations that use these methods more dynamic. Successful organizations of the future will obviously also serve global markets characterized by differing consumer preferences from the present and increasing product specialization. Early in this new millennium, it has been predicted, revenues from outside the home country market will overtake domestic sales for many organizations as the global market expands rapidly. Organizations must gauge future growth opportunities with these emerging markets in mind.

Organizations in the future must also focus on changes in the labor market. Employees will be, on average, younger and more technically literate than today's workers, and they will exemplify modern attitudes toward the employer-employee relationship. They will tend to change jobs more frequently, and their loyalty to employers will be predicated on opportunities for interesting and challenging work that stretches their capabilities. The employees' knowledge and experience will directly relate to the employer's major sources of competitive advantage ("core competencies") and the size and elasticity of the employer's associated labor markets. Additionally, a large and growing share of employees may reside outside of the country in which the corporation makes its headquarters.

Given these factors and based on a review of literature and experiences in the corporate world, Pattanayak (2001) has suggested a new model for corporate excellence. The assessment presented here is based on the ten-attribute model, which is shown in Figure 1.

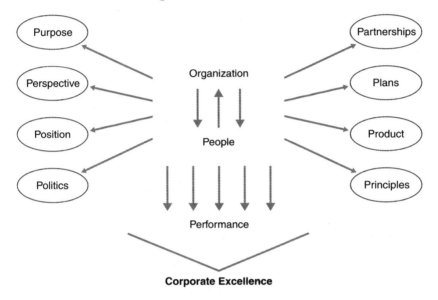

Figure 1.   Ten Dimensions of Corporate Excellence

THE MODEL OF CORPORATE EXCELLENCE

As shown in Figure 1, corporate excellence can be seen as a combination of people, systems, products, and marketing excellence, resulting in ten separate dimensions: purpose, perspective, position, politics, partnership, planning, product, principles, people, and performance.

The ten dimensions can be defined as follows:

- *Purpose* is the goal, vision, or business aim of the organization.
- *Perspective* is the direction an organization is taking, a mental view of the relative state of what is happening at any point.

- *Position* is the image of the company seen from outside, as in its position within its marketplace.

- *Politics* is the judicious and expedient behavior of people within the organization.

- *Partnership* is the state of being a partner or partners, to be a part of the organization.

- *Plans* are the plans of action taken by the organization as a whole and by the work groups.

- *Product* is the innovative, augmented, cost-effective output.

- *Principles* are the set of values, culture, and philosophy by which the organization functions.

- *People* are challenging, ethical, committed, high performers and self-driven.

- *Performance* is the result.

When completing the Ten P's: Assessing Corporate Excellence assessment, respondents evaluate the degree to which the ten dimensions of corporate excellence are present in their organization using a five-point Likert scale.

DESCRIPTION AND ADMINISTRATION OF THE INSTRUMENT

The instrument consists of eighty-nine statements. It can be administered individually or in groups, irrespective of the departments to which the respondents belong as long as they are all members of the same organization. The instructions are provided at the beginning of the instrument. The facilitator should give everyone a copy and a pen or pencil, then read through the instructions, reminding respondents to answer based on their own view of the organization *at the present time,* not any planned future or past time frame. They should circle the number that best represents their views.

RELIABILITY AND VALIDITY

The reliability of this instrument was calculated through split-half method for internal consistency after administering the scale with two hundred executives. The Cronbach alpha for the inventory was 0.89. The correlation of all the dimensions to the total score ranged from 0.52 to 0.83, respectively.

The item validity of the inventory was found through factor analysis to determine whether items measured what they were intended to measure. The final items were selected on the basis of factor loading and the correlation coefficient (r) of each item with the total score. Two items were removed, after which 100 percent of the variance was accounted for by the ten dimensions.

SCORING AND INTERPRETATION

Respondents can be asked to total their points for each of the dimensions. Note that on the Scoring Sheet scores must be reversed for the negatively worded items (5, 12, 14, 31, 33, 34, 38, 39, 53, 61, and 62). All the items are rated on the five-point Likert scale shown below, and scores are subtotaled for each factor/dimension.

> 5= Strongly Agree; 4 = Agree; 3 = Uncertain;
> 2 = Disagree and 1= Strongly Disagree.

After they have scored their assessments, have respondents put their scores on the Data Collection Sheet for discussion of the company's Ten P's in the large group.

SUGGESTED USES

The instrument is useful for gathering information about attributes in organizations. It can also identify critical problem areas in companies that are desirous of attaining excellence in the future. Respondents can discuss any dimension that has a low average score by looking at the individual items that make up the dimension. The group can work together to come up with action plans for changing the organization with regard to that particular dimension. It is recommended that the assessment be given again at a later time to check for improvement.

References

Kaplan, R.S., & Norton, D.P. (1992, January/February). The balanced scorecard: Measures that drive performance. *Harvard Business Review,* pp. 71-79.

Kaplan, R.S., & Norton, D.P. (1996, January/February). Using the balanced scorecards as a strategic management system. *Harvard Business Review,* pp. 75-85.

Pattanayak, B.(2001). Human resource perspectives in corporate excellence: A proposed model. *Indian Journal of Industrial Relations, 36*(3), 345–353.

Peters, T. (1988). *In search of excellence.* New York: Warner.

Schmidt, J.A (1999, November/December). Corporate excellence in the new millennium. *The Journal of Business Strategy, 20*(6), 39–43.

Biswajeet Pattanayak, Ph.D., *is the director of the North Eastern Institute of Bank Management in India. He was previously a professor of human resource management and organizational behavior. He holds a Ph.D. and D.Litt. in industrial and organization psychology and is a Fellow of the All India Management Association, New Delhi, with more than thirteen years of experience both in industry and academia. He has conducted management development programs and consultancy assignments for public, private, and multinational companies, including the World Bank. He has authored fourteen books and more than sixty research publications.*

Rajnish Kumar Misra *is lecturer in the Symbiosis Centre for HRD, Pune. He has over five years of experience both in industry and academia.*

Phalgu Niranjana *is a research associate in IIM Indore and also pursuing her Ph.D. degree from Utkal University, Bhubaneshwar, India.*

Sanjyot Pethe, Ph.D., *is currently senior lecturer in the Nirma Institute of Management, Ahemdabad, India, and has over five years of teaching experience in organizational behavior and human resources.*

Ten P's: Assessing Corporate Excellence

Biswajeet Pattanayak, Rajnish Kumar Misra, Phalgu Niranjana, and Sanjyot Pethe

Instructions: The statements below reflect various dimensions of organizational practices. Read each one carefully and circle the response that is true for the statement as it pertains to *your* organization at the present time.

1 = Strongly Agree   2 = Agree   3 = Uncertain   4 = Disagree   5 = Strongly Disagree

I. Purpose

1. The goals of this organization have been identified after careful analysis of our competitors.	1	2	3	4	5
2. Employees are aware of the goals of the organization.	1	2	3	4	5
3. This organization fixes/freezes its annual targets in consonance with its business policy.	1	2	3	4	5
4. The vision of the organization is to become an excellent place to work, grow, and develop.	1	2	3	4	5
5. The employees do not know the targets of this organization.	1	2	3	4	5
6. The organization has a clearly defined vision.	1	2	3	4	5
7. The purpose to the organization is well-defined.	1	2	3	4	5
8. All members of this organization are aware of its purpose.	1	2	3	4	5
9. All members of this organization identify with the purpose of this organization.	1	2	3	4	5
10. All members of this organization accept its corporate vision.	1	2	3	4	5

II. Perspective

11. Most activities of this organization are aligned with the organizational goals.	1	2	3	4	5

12. Employees are not clear about the activities
they are expected to do.   1   2   3   4   5

13. The organization prioritizes its activities
according to targets/goals to be achieved.   1   2   3   4   5

14. Employees in this organization have no
clear-cut roles.   1   2   3   4   5

15. Employees have well-defined procedures
to work within this organization.   1   2   3   4   5

16. Policies are clearly defined and provide
clear guidelines.   1   2   3   4   5

III. Position

17. The products of the organization are liked
by the customers.   1   2   3   4   5

18. The organization has a very good reputation
in the market.   1   2   3   4   5

19. This organization is able to meet the
expectations of its customers.   1   2   3   4   5

20. This organization possesses a large customer
base in its market.   1   2   3   4   5

21. This organization frequently compares itself
with other organizations to remain competitive.   1   2   3   4   5

22. This organization is sensitive to the changing
demands of customers.   1   2   3   4   5

23. This organization is known to be environ-
mentally friendly.   1   2   3   4   5

24. This organization is known to be quality-
conscious.   1   2   3   4   5

25. This organization aligns its activities with
customer demands.   1   2   3   4   5

26. This organization responds to its customers'
needs.   1   2   3   4   5

27. This organization continuously upgrades
    itself in terms of technology.   1   2   3   4   5

28. This organization is known for its employee-
    friendly practices.   1   2   3   4   5

IV. Politics

29. Employees are treated equally in this
    organization.   1   2   3   4   5

30. Superiors reward their subordinates for their
    contributions in achieving organizational
    targets.   1   2   3   4   5

31. Promotions are given to those who are able
    to influence their superiors, not necessarily
    because of their merit.   1   2   3   4   5

32. People in this organization are rewarded for
    their high performance.   1   2   3   4   5

33. People indulge in flattery to earn their
    superiors' favor.   1   2   3   4   5

34. Groups indulge in activities to corner large
    gains for themselves.   1   2   3   4   5

35. Groups share the resources for achieving
    organizational goals.   1   2   3   4   5

36. People in this organization trust one another. 1   2   3   4   5

37. People in this organization help each other
    as and when the need arises.   1   2   3   4   5

38. Subordinates insinuate themselves with
    superiors to receive promotions.   1   2   3   4   5

39. Employees who are associated with important
    people in the organization are perceived
    as powerful themselves.   1   2   3   4   5

40. Resource allocation in this organization is
    based on job demands.   1   2   3   4   5

V. Partnerships

41. Extensive collaboration occurs between various teams and departments in achieving organizational goals.   1   2   3   4   5

42. This organization joins with other organizations to capitalize on opportunities.   1   2   3   4   5

43. People work together in this organization to identify future challenges.   1   2   3   4   5

44. People here are allowed to design strategies for introducing innovative products.   1   2   3   4   5

45. Mutual dependency is recognized by every member of the organization.   1   2   3   4   5

46. Roles in this organization are negotiated with the person filling the role.   1   2   3   4   5

47. Employees involve themselves in various activities of the organization.   1   2   3   4   5

48. Employees are able to respond to customers freely.   1   2   3   4   5

VI. Plans

49. Decisions about launching new products are made after careful market analysis.   1   2   3   4   5

50. The organization can take an idea and quickly turn it into a product that people want to buy.   1   2   3   4   5

51. Plans are drawn that involve cross-functional teams.   1   2   3   4   5

52. The organization draws short-term and long-term plans for strategic action.   1   2   3   4   5

53. The organization is unable to achieve goals most of the time due to lack of proper planning.   1   2   3   4   5

VII. Product

54. Before launching a new product, the organization plans properly.   1   2   3   4   5

55. Products of this company add value for the customers.   1   2   3   4   5

56. Our products ensure good service.   1   2   3   4   5

57. This organization has good after-sales service for its customers.   1   2   3   4   5

58. New products are intermittently introduced to broaden the customer base.   1   2   3   4   5

59. Our qualitative products and services command customer loyalty.   1   2   3   4   5

VIII. Principles

60. Our organization has a transparent policy for decision making and communication.   1   2   3   4   5

61. Hard work and commitment are not recognized in this organization.   1   2   3   4   5

62. There are no clearly defined systems and procedures in this organization.   1   2   3   4   5

63. This company has a strong, value-based system of working.   1   2   3   4   5

64. Top management's leadership style reflects the values being practiced in this organization.   1   2   3   4   5

65. Employees discuss problems among themselves in order to solve them.   1   2   3   4   5

66. This organization closely monitors the target achievements of each employee.   1   2   3   4   5

67. The organization is concerned about the development of its people.   1   2   3   4   5

68. Taking responsibility for tasks outside of one's normal role is recognized and rewarded.   1   2   3   4   5

69. The culture of the organization is such that
high performers are automatically recognized.   1   2   3   4   5

70. The organization rewards its employees for
their ethical practices.   1   2   3   4   5

IX. People

71. Employees are empowered to take initiative.   1   2   3   4   5

72. People in this organization are open to change.   1   2   3   4   5

73. Employees here can obtain management
support to implement initiatives.   1   2   3   4   5

74. Top management inspires people to be
innovative.   1   2   3   4   5

75. Employees are praised for their success in
taking initiative.   1   2   3   4   5

76. The organization takes care of the employees'
needs.   1   2   3   4   5

77. Employees are rewarded here for their
good work.   1   2   3   4   5

78. People in this organization are able to utilize
available resources.   1   2   3   4   5

79. People in this organization identify with
the goals of the organization.   1   2   3   4   5

80. Continuous feedback is given to the employ-
ees in order to facilitate their development.   1   2   3   4   5

81. People are aware of their competencies and
use them accordingly.   1   2   3   4   5

82. High performers are rewarded in this
organization.   1   2   3   4   5

83. Human values are respected in this
organization.   1   2   3   4   5

84. People in this organization are highly
committed to their work assignments.   1   2   3   4   5

1 = Strongly Agree   2 = Agree   3 = Uncertain   4 = Disagree   5 = Strongly Disagree

X. Performance

85. Employees' willingness to put in extra
    effort is very high, irrespective of reward
    and recognition.   1   2   3   4   5

86. This organization is able to set its own
    benchmarks.   1   2   3   4   5

87. This organization is highly productive
    because of its realistic targets.   1   2   3   4   5

88. In this organization, performance ratings
    are based both on quality and on the
    quantity of results.   1   2   3   4   5

89. Rewards and promotions are performance-
    based in this organization.   1   2   3   4   5

THE TEN P'S SCORING SHEET

Instructions: Transfer your scores for each of the numbered items to the form below and total by section. Note that the scores for some of the items must be reversed. These items have an asterisk beside them. Transfer the scores very carefully for these items. Next, transfer your total scores to the Data Collection Sheet and make notes in preparation for discussing places your organization could make improvements.

Item No	Score	Item No	Score	Item No	Score
I. 1		III. 17		34*	
2		18		35	
3		19		36	
4		20		37	
5*		21		38*	
6		22		39*	
7		23		40	
8		24		Total	
9		25		V. 41	
10		26		42	
Total		27		43	
II. 11		28		44	
12*		Total		45	
13		IV. 29		46	
14*		30		47	
15		31*		48	
16		32		Total	
Total		33*			

*Reverse the score for these items.

Item No	Score	Item No	Score	Item No	Score
VI. 49		VIII. 60		76	
50		61*		77	
51		62*		78	
52		63		79	
53*		64		80	
Total		65		81	
VII. 54		66		82	
55		67		83	
56		68		84	
57		69		Total	
58		70		X. 85	
59		Total		86	
Total		IX. 71		87	
		72		88	
		73		89	
		74		Total	
		75			

Ten P's Data Collection Sheet

	Dimensions	Minimum Score	Maximum Score	Your Score
I.	Purpose	10	50	
II.	Perspective	6	30	
III.	Position	12	60	
IV.	Politics	12	60	
V.	Partnerships	8	40	
VI.	Plans	5	25	
VII.	Product	6	30	
VIII.	Principles	11	55	
IX.	People	14	70	
X.	Performance	5	25	

Introduction
to the Presentation and Discussion Resources Section

The Presentation and Discussion Resources Section is a collection of articles of use to every facilitator. The theories, background information, models, and methods will challenge facilitators' thinking, enrich their professional development, and assist their internal and external clients with productive change. These articles may be used as a basis for lecturettes, as handouts in training sessions, or as background reading material.

This section will provide you with a variety of useful ideas, theoretical opinions, teachable models, practical strategies, and proven intervention methods. The articles will add richness and depth to your training and consulting knowledge and skills. They will challenge you to think differently, explore new concepts, and experiment with new interventions. The articles will continue to add a fresh perspective to your work.

The 2003 Annual: Volume 2, Consulting includes nine articles in the following categories:

Individual Development: Developing Awareness and Understanding

Be Worth a Million at Work, by Peter R. Garber

Communication: Clarity and Precision in Communication

Look Who's Talking! The Power of Nonverbal Communication, by Judith A. Colbert

Communication: Coaching and Encouraging

Coaching for Results: An Overview of Effective Tools, by Marcia Ruben and Jan M. Schmuckler

Communication: Technology

Understanding the Online Context, by Heidi A. Campbell

Groups and Teams: Group Development

To Team Well or Not to Team at All: That Is the Question, by Marlene Caroselli

Groups and Teams: Techniques to Use with Groups

Leveraging Difference and Diversity in Multicultural Teams, Virtually or Face-to-Face, by Dianne Hofner Saphiere

Consulting: OD Theory and Practice

Future Areas Beckoning Partnerships Between Human Resource Professionals and Industrial/Organizational Psychologists, by Robert T. Brill

Consulting: Consulting Strategies and Techniques

The ABC's of Strategic Management℠: The Systems Thinking Approach℠ to Creating a Customer-Focused, High-Performance Organization, by Stephen G. Haines

Leadership: Top-Management Issues and Concerns

How to Retain High-Performance Employees, by Beverly Kaye and Sharon Jordan-Evans

As with previous *Annuals,* this volume covers a wide variety of topics. The range of articles presented encourages thought-provoking discussion about the present and future of HRD. Other articles on specific subjects can be located by using our comprehensive *Reference Guide to Handbooks and Annuals.* The guide is updated regularly and indexes the contents of all the *Annuals* and the *Handbooks of Structured Experiences.* With each revision, the *Reference Guide* becomes a complete, up-to-date, and easy-to-use resource for selecting appropriate materials from the *Annuals* and *Handbooks.* A print version of the *Reference Guide* is available for volumes through 1999. An online supplement covering the years through 2003 can be found at www.pfeiffer.com/go/supplement.

Here and in the *Reference Guide,* we have done our best to categorize the articles for easy reference; however, many of the articles encompass a range of topics, disciplines, and applications. If you do not find what you are looking for under one category, check a related category. In some cases we may place an article in the "Training" *Annual* that also has implications for "Consulting," and vice versa. As the field of HRD continues to grow and develop, there is more and more crossover between training and consulting. Explore all the contents of both volumes of the *Annual* in order to realize the full potential for learning and development that each offers.

BE WORTH A MILLION AT WORK

Peter R. Garber

Abstract: This article examines the meaning of worth
and value. Although many people equate value with
money, many other things in life are also of value.
Playing off the format of the game show, "Who
Wants to Be a Millionaire?," the author presents a variety of analogies to consider that could elevate one's
self-worth, both personally and professionally.

What Is Really of Value?

Shown by the enormous popularity of the TV game show, "Who Wants to Be a Millionaire?" there is a great deal of speculation on how it would feel to suddenly win a million dollars. In just a few minutes, average people are headed toward millionaire status—as long as they can keep their "lifelines" intact before they get to the really big money questions. If only their Aunt Alice or best friend Harry knows the answer to a question like the following, they could win that coveted million dollars:

1. Who did Bill Clinton defeat in the 1996 presidential election?

   A. George Bush

   B. George W. Bush

   C. Bob Dole

   D. Ronald Reagan

Now let's think about the value of what you know in a different way. Consider how much you're worth at work. Not how much you are currently being paid, as this may or may not be an accurate reflection of your actual value to the organization. Placing an accurate monetary value on something as subjective as one's contributions at work may be impossible, but just for argument's sake, take a guess. Think about what value you bring to your employer's business or goals. Is this value more or less than what you are currently being paid? It is likely that the majority of people who answer this question would say that their services are worth more than what they are paid, and in many cases it would be true.

But keep in mind that a major reason that you are employed is to help your employer reach his or her goals. This leads to job security for both you and your employer. Of course, this is not to say that you should turn down that next raise.

What can you do to increase your value on the job? Why should you worry that you are worth more than you are being paid? Wouldn't working harder for the same amount of money just feed the corporate greed you hear so much about today? Why should you try to increase the value of your contributions without an increase in salary? The answers to these questions are as diverse as the people who ponder such things. However, one common reason shared by many is pride. People invest a great deal of themselves both professionally and personally in their careers. They are rightfully proud of what they accomplish. Their pride serves to motivate them to work hard to meet organizational goals, even without commensurate salary increases.

Being worth a million at work equates to the personal pride and satisfaction one receives through doing the work itself. Everything else is a bonus.

This article was written not to help you make more money nor to teach you techniques for negotiating a big raise, but to help you feel good about your work—and ultimately about yourself.

Your life is more than a job, and your happiness should not depend on the successes or failures you might have at work, but much of your identity and a great deal of time may be intertwined in what you do for a living. Your job determines in large measure your lifestyle, peer group, social status, financial security, and so forth. Balancing work and personal responsibilities is perhaps the most valuable skill that one can learn.

Unfortunately, reaching this balance can be one of the hardest goals for many people. They may feel compelled to expend nearly all of their energies and time on their careers. They do this in the erroneous belief that their efforts are for their families and their futures. In reality, they are investing themselves and their time unwisely. To reach the pinnacle of success in your career only to diminish the value of the relationships of those closest to you would be a very hollow accomplishment. The true riches from work come from meeting your responsibilities in all aspects of your life, not just focusing on your career.

On the flip side, employers must be aware that they employ the whole person, but only for the portion of time that person spends at work. The more personally and professionally fulfilled the individual, ultimately the more productive he or she will be to the company.

By the way, the correct answer to the million-dollar question is "C. Bob Dole." Would you have gone home a millionaire?

It's Your Turn

Imagine that you have just been given the opportunity of a lifetime. Such opportunities probably pass your way nearly every day. You just have to be able to recognize them when they appear.

Opportunities often are disguised as problems or interruptions in our lives. Consequently, we try to ignore them or make them go away. Or it may seem like other people are getting all the breaks or best assignments. You can either focus all of your energies on worrying about what you think other people have or you can make the most of the opportunities that do come your way. The choice is ultimately yours.

Timing is critical. At certain times you may be called on to perform at higher levels than you ever have before. At these times, you must *step up to the plate* and perform to the best of your ability. These are the times when it is *your turn* to make a difference. Usually, the window of opportunity is open for a very brief moment and quickly closes again. See these opportunities for what they really are and be able to capitalize on them. You may not have another turn.

The next time a challenge is presented to you, look at it as an opportunity, not as a problem. Think of it as your turn to make a difference. Make the most of this opportunity. It just might lead you to the really big payoff that you have been seeking.

Which of the following describes how opportunities in your career often present themselves?

A. As a problem or interruption

B. As a sure bet

C. As a rare occurrence

D. As something you can act on any time

The correct answer is A.

IN THE HOT SEAT

Sometimes the pressure is really on. Just as on "Who Wants to Be a Millionaire?," all eyes are focused on you and you are called on to make extremely important decisions. The good news is that you probably aren't called to sit in the hot seat very often. However, the decisions you make and actions you take while there may have a dramatic effect on the rest of your career—and ultimately your life.

It is always easier to watch someone else sit in the hot seat and be critical of his or her decisions. "I knew better than that," we might say to ourselves when we hear someone choose an incorrect answer. But if we were to be in that situation, the right answers might not be so easy to find. Instead of criticizing other people (which would add no value), we should instead be asking ourselves how we might be able to help. You could become a *lifeline* of sorts. Although the person must make the final decision for him- or herself, it is always reassuring to hear input from others.

How can you prepare for when you will have to sit in the hot seat yourself? It may not be possible to be totally prepared, as in envisioning the problems beforehand. But what you learn and experience on the job prepares you a little bit each day for the critical decisions you will have to make later. Pay attention to life's lessons. Think of every challenge or problem you face as a learning opportunity. Grow from these experiences and learn what you can from them. These might become the most valuable assets that you ever acquire. You may find yourself in the hot seat someday and may be able to answer all the questions correctly. Who knows what your experiences may be worth to you?

Which of the following might be an example of being in the hot seat at work?

A. *When everything is going fine*

B. *When everyone is agreeing with you*

C. *When you have a very difficult decision to make*

D. *When the choices are easy*

The correct answer is C.

REACHING OUT

Lifelines provide players on "Who Wants to Be a Millionaire?" the opportunity to reach out to other people for help. Contestants can poll the audience, ask for a 50/50 (in which two of the incorrect answers are eliminated), or telephone a friend.

In life, we face many questions each day for which we want the help of others. Sometimes the answers may not be apparent, even to those from whom we seek advice. But the very process of reaching out serves other beneficial purposes. The support of others when dealing with the difficult questions in life is often a first step toward solving the problems.

There is an old saying, "The only dumb question is the one that isn't asked." Unfortunately, we often feel embarrassed to ask questions if we think others would expect us to know the answers. But we cause ourselves even greater embarrassment by not asking questions. Reaching out for help not only gives us the benefits of another's knowledge and experience, but it makes that person feel good that we respected his or her opinion enough to ask for it. Don't be afraid to reach out to others. The best thing about these lifelines in real life is that we are not limited to three.

Which of the following would be an example of using a lifeline at work?

A. *Examining a bill from a supplier*

B. *Taking extra work from the boss*

C. *Seeking advice from a co-worker*

D. *Finding a lost computer password*

The correct answer is C.

LIVING WITH YOUR DECISIONS

Our decisions often have far-reaching implications for our lives. And many of our decisions are irrevocable. They are our *final answers*. Right or wrong, we have no choice but to live with the decisions that we make.

Decisions of this magnitude must be made carefully and thoughtfully. We shouldn't allow ourselves to be rushed without thinking through all of the implications. There may be more at stake than money. The consequences may be of greater importance and value than any sum of money. You can't really put a price tag on such things as your happiness or relationships with others.

Make your decisions carefully and be prepared to live with the consequences, whatever they might be. Everything happens for a reason, and our decisions, right or wrong, lead us along life's pathways.

Which of the following best describes the consequences of the decisions you make in life?

A. *Irrevocable*

B. *Easily changed*

C. *Easy*

D. *Always correct*

The correct answer is A.

Strategies of the Game

Sports teams always go into a game with a strategy for winning called a game plan. Without such a plan, a team would be at a disadvantage in relation to the competition, who would come prepared with their own plan. A team could be as much as defeated before it even stepped on the field.

Even contestants on the millionaire show have strategies. They may choose to play conservatively, taking few risks. They might decide, once they have reached a certain level of success, that they don't want to jeopardize it with an incorrect answer and lose what they have already won. Others may have a completely different strategy and be more willing to take risks. Much strategy is based on the player's overall objective for playing the game. If the person's strategy is to win the million dollars, then he or she must take more risks than someone who would be satisfied to go home with a lesser amount.

What is your strategy or game plan? Do you even have one? Many people would have to answer that they do not have a strategy for their careers. But without such a plan, you might find yourself having to accept whatever happens. You would be at a great disadvantage compared to someone who has developed a strategy and game plan for his or her future. Developing such a plan helps you to capitalize on future opportunities in your career. Knowing what you want to do and creating a strategy for achieving your goals is half the battle for realizing your dreams.

Having a strategy for your future career will do which of the following?

A. Guarantee your future success

B. Help guide you toward your goals

C. Make everyone at work angry with you

D. Force you into early retirement

The correct answer is B.

No Guarantees

On "Who Wants to Be a Millionaire?," there are no guarantees that anyone will win the top prize money—or anything at all. Contestants earn money by playing the game correctly and by making the right decisions. This is also true in the game of life. There are no guarantees that you will be successful. You must earn your success each and every day, playing by the rules and making good choices.

But you can increase your chances of being successful in your career. The best way to do this is the old-fashioned way—*you have to earn it.* There is no substitute for hard work and dedication to your job. And although hard work and dedication won't guarantee success, without them the chances of your getting ahead will be much less.

Without some amount of hard work and dedication, you will not be successful—unless, of course, you are given the opportunity of a lifetime and are picked out of millions of viewers to appear on a television show and win a million dollars. Unfortunately, few of us will ever have this chance, so we need to focus our energies instead on those things that can maximize our chances for success. We need to work on the *sure bets* in life. There usually are no short-cuts. And that, ultimately, is the final answer.

What is the only way to guarantee that you can be successful at work?

A. Hard work and dedication

B. Faking it

C. Pretending you know things that you don't

D. Back-stabbing

The correct answer is A.

Easy Questions/Difficult Choices

Sometimes the seemingly easiest questions are actually the most difficult because we don't give them enough thought. This can be a very big mistake. Have you ever seen a contestant on the show hurriedly answer one of the "easy" questions without really understanding what was asked? The person sits confidently, waiting for Regis to congratulate him or her for picking the correct answer. Instead, the person is shown the way off stage with all three lifelines still intact. If only these contestants had thought before they answered or had asked for help, they would have had a chance for the big money.

To increase your chances for success at work, you can't take anything for granted. The questions you face may appear to be easy but actually be difficult or complex. There are often many levels of interpretation. Make sure you really understand what is being asked before answering. Most important is to understand what other people think the question is. You might be surprised just how different their perceptions of the problem are from yours.

The bottom line is that there really aren't any easy answers in life. You need to take every question seriously and fully understand it. It will save you many problems as well as keep you in the game of life.

Which is the best way to answer what appears to be an easy question?

A. Quickly

B. By ignoring it

C. After careful consideration

D. Without anyone's help

The correct answer is C.

AUDIENCE REACTION

How the audience reacts to a contestant can have a dramatic effect on how well he or she performs. Although the audience is not permitted to help the contestants, their influence can be felt by their reactions to the potential answers. Sometimes the audience even gets to play a more active role by being polled as one of a player's three lifelines. Usually the audience provides the contestant with good advice, helping him or her get past the question to the bigger money ahead.

Life may not always come with a live audience, but many people play important parts in our lives. And as on the "Who Wants to Be a Millionaire?" show, they may not participate in every decision we make, but their opinions are still very important. Sometimes they may be noticeably quiet, but they are still concerned about us and our future. Watch and listen closely to the reactions of those who are in the *audience* of your life. Their reactions can give you some of the most valuable guidance you will ever receive.

What should you do about the reactions of other people in your life?

A. Ignore those reactions

B. Do the opposite of what they think

C. Pay close attention to what others think

D. Tell other people to mind their own business

The correct answer is C.

Good Luck

Just how big a part does luck play in career success? And why is it that some people seem to have all the luck? What enables one person to rise to the top of his or her profession while others with just as much talent and ability end up struggling all their lives? Why does lady luck shine benevolently on some people and seem to have the opposite effect on others? These are all questions that are impossible to answer. But one thing is sure: If you depend entirely on luck, you are headed for certain disappointment.

You truly do make your own luck in life. Certainly, we all need to have things go our way once in a while. You could call this luck. But if we don't put ourselves in a situation in the first place, we won't be in the position to be the benefactor of luck. Luck isn't something that just falls in our laps—we help to create it. Many years of hard work prepare us for that lucky day to come.

Perhaps someday you will be given the chance to win a million dollars on a TV game show. When given that chance of a lifetime, maybe you will be lucky enough to be given questions on topics that you (or your lifelines) are knowledgeable about. But then again, this may never happen. Instead, you will have to rely on the everyday opportunities that come your way. You need to recognize just how lucky you are to have the opportunities you do have. The most successful people do.

Which of the following best describes how to be lucky?

A. Carry a rabbit's foot

B. Wear lucky socks (and never wash them)

C. Make the most of everyday opportunities

D. Keep your fingers crossed

The correct answer is C.

Cashing In

Players on the millionaire show often decide to take what they have already won and go home rather than risk it. They cash in their chance at becoming an instant millionaire for something they have for sure. Of course, this decision is arrived at with a great deal of anguish and usually comes after the player is presented with a question for which he or she is unsure of the answer.

The real question is whether it is better to go for a sure bet or to risk everything for something of greater value. Like contestants on the show, we make decisions like this all the time, probably every day at work. Unlike on the show, where players are immediately told how their decisions would have turned out, we usually have to wait to learn the results of ours. It is likely that we may never know for sure what *would have been* if we had decided differently.

How do you make these kinds of decisions? Do you weigh all of the facts at hand, as well as seek the advice of everyone you can? Do you consider what you have to lose compared with what you have to gain? Are you comfortable that you can live with the consequences of your decision either way? These are all factors you must take into consideration when making important decisions in your career. Be it cashing in on a sure bet or taking a risk in your career, the consequences may not always cost you a million dollars but are still very important to your life. Make these decisions carefully and thoughtfully.

What factors should you consider when making important career decisions?

A. The risks

B. The advice and opinions of others

C. How comfortable you are with your decision

D. All of these answers

The correct answer is D.

PAYING THE TAXES

There really is no such thing as a free lunch, not even on a television game show. Even those who are lucky enough to leave with a million dollars will pay a significant portion of their winnings to the tax collector. Unfortunately, taxes are one of the few certainties in life, a way of paying our dues for all the things that we receive.

There are other forms of "taxes" that we must pay in our careers as well. These may not require cash, but extract a cost just the same, such as the hard work and sacrifices that you have had to make to get to the position in life where you are today. Nothing comes without a price tag, including your future goals.

It would be unrealistic to expect to get ahead in life without paying some kind of price for success. You will pay these "taxes" as you climb the corporate ladder. You might pay your taxes a little at a time or all at once but, ultimately, they have to be paid.

Taxes in your career might be best compared to which of the following?

A. *All your hard work and sacrifice to be successful*

B. *A free parking space*

C. *Extra cheese on your pizza*

D. *Keys to the executive washroom*

The correct answer is A.

THE PRESSURE IS ON

The lights are dimmed; the music becomes more intense; there is an eerie silence in the studio. Even Regis is quiet as the contestant agonizes over what might be the right answer to the million-dollar question. If only he hadn't squandered his lifelines on those earlier questions. Now he is truly on his own and, although millions of viewers are watching at home, he has never felt more alone in his life. He is almost positive he knows the correct answer, but is he sure enough to risk what he has already won? On the other hand, does he really want to turn his back on an additional half-million dollars? When would he ever have another chance to take home so much money for answering just one question? He is almost positive that he knows the answer. Now this is pressure!

The more that is a stake, the greater the pressure becomes to be successful. This is true both for contestants on "Who Wants to Be a Millionaire?" as they move ahead to the bigger money questions and for us as we progress in our careers. More responsibility usually means greater pressure at work. How we react to this pressure can mean the difference between being successful in our careers and not reaching our goals. Pressure is a double-edged sword. In one instance it can help motivate you to perform at the top of your game and to the best of your abilities. At other times it might be more detrimental, causing you to succumb to its influence and not perform to your usual standards.

Learning to deal with pressure is essential to success in any endeavor. Sometimes it is simply a matter of experience and getting used to working under stressful circumstances. It is also a matter of confidence. If you are sure you know the answer, you will feel less pressure. Learning as much as you can about your job will not only make you more valuable at work but also reduce the pressure on you.

Learning to deal with the pressures you have to face at work is usually a matter of which of the following?

A. Blaming problems on others

B. Covering up your mistakes

C. Ignoring problems

D. Learning and experience

The correct answer is D.

TIMING

In our economy today, fortunes can be made or lost in the blink of an eye. Often it is just a matter of timing. As they say, it helps to be in the right place at the right time. It is also important to have an understanding of when certain things need to be done. There seems to be a time and a place for everything. Having a better understanding of the timing can make the difference between making a fortune and losing everything. Timing may not be everything, but it comes in a close second in the race for success.

Timing in many ways seems to be a lot like luck. It may be out of your control but it still has an enormous influence over your future success. But, like luck, do you make your own timing? Can you actually put yourself in the right place at the right time? Do contestants on "Who Wants to Be a Millionaire?" enable themselves to be in the right place at just the right time to win a million dollars? The answer is that they did do something to put themselves in this fortunate position. They overcame all of the obstacles in their way to being invited to sit in the million-dollar hot seat.

How can you create your own good timing at work? How can you ensure that you are in the right place at the right time to take advantage of the opportunities that might come your way? What obstacles do you need to overcome to be in line for that which is most valuable to you in your career?

Timing in your career is a matter of which of the following?

A. Overcoming obstacles

B. Luck

C. Being in the wrong place

D. Being late

The correct answer is A.

BANKRUPTCY

The opposite of becoming a millionaire might be going bankrupt. Contestants can go bankrupt by failing to get to the minimum level of prize money, one thousand dollars. They not only miss the opportunity of a lifetime to take home a million dollars, but they fail to win any money at all. This typically happens because they don't really listen carefully enough to the question and make a hasty decision.

Going bankrupt in real life may involve this same kind of mistake. Becoming bankrupt may also be a metaphor for losing other valuable things in life. For example, one can become emotionally bankrupt, drained of emotions to a critical level. This type of bankruptcy can be the most devastating of all. Like missing one of the early questions on the millionaire show, bankruptcy often comes about because one doesn't think through a decision. Once the person sees the error, he or she would do anything to have the opportunity to answer again. But his or her turn is over.

Which of the following is a possible reason for someone to end up bankrupt in some manner at work?

A. Not listening to what is being asked of one

B. Paying attention to details

C. Making wise investments of time

D. Maintaining good relationships with co-workers

The correct answer is A.

The Questions Become Harder

As the stakes grow higher, the questions always seem to get harder and harder. This is true both in game shows and in life. As you move forward in your career, everything tends to become more complex. Problems become more multi-dimensional with complicated possibilities for each solution. Your responsibilities grow as you take on new roles with greater accountabilities. The pressure increases as you face these greater challenges, testing your ability to keep your composure.

But along with increased responsibilities, the rewards will also increase. Such rewards can come in many different forms. Of course, you would expect a raise or some other form of financial incentive, but the rewards for increased responsibility may not come in the form of money. Other rewards that may have an even greater and longer impact on your life include the personal satisfaction and pride you gain by overcoming the challenges. These are perhaps the most valuable paybacks for taking on increased responsibilities and challenges in life.

As you move ahead in your career, what tends to happen to the questions and problems you face each day?

A. They get easier

B. You can ignore more of them

C. People become less interested

D. They become harder and harder

The correct answer is D

Support Systems

Our support systems are the lifelines that we depend on every day. Fortunately, in real life we are not limited to just three, as contestants are on the show. These support systems include important people in our lives who provide guidance to us in many ways on a daily basis. We may ask them directly for help or simply may depend on their encouragement and on knowing that they are there for us. Best of all, we are not limited to just one call!

Sometimes on the show, a player loses by incorrectly answering a question before using even one of the lifelines. Perhaps the person's strategy was to save the lifelines until the later questions, but by not reaching out for help when it was needed, the player never had an opportunity to get to that point.

The lesson to learn from this is that when you need help you shouldn't be reluctant to ask for it. That's what your support systems or lifelines are there for. Use them when you need them. Don't wait until it is too late for anyone to be able to help you. The people who provide support for you would much rather you come to them for help *before* you have a big problem, rather than later, when there may be little or nothing they can do for you.

When should you ask for help from those who can provide support to you?

A. When you have a big problem

B. Before you have a problem

C. After it is too late

D. Never

The correct answer is B.

THE REAL MILLIONAIRES

The real question is: "What is most important in your life?" Finding the answer can help you better manage your life. In the final analysis, few people would look back on their lives and say, "Gee, I wish that I had spent more time at the office!" The wisdom of time teaches us what is really important and how to balance our many priorities. Becoming a millionaire in the game of life involves much more than just accumulating money or material goods. The true riches are much less tangible. That which is of the greatest value is the most difficult to acquire. No amount of money in the world can replace or buy these things, nor can you win them on a television game show. These riches are the relationships we have with other people, both at work and in our personal lives.

Nurture these relationships and help them grow stronger. They will pay you greater dividends than any other investment you could ever make. The real millionaires are those who realize the true value of their relationships with others.

The real riches in life are in the form of which of the following?

A. The relationships we have with others

B. Stocks and bonds

C. Material possessions

D. Bonus plans

The correct answer is A.

Final Answers

"Is that your *final* answer?" has become the latest cliché as a result of the popularity of the show. But it is a very good question to ask yourself when making any important decision, be it at work or in your personal life. That little voice inside your head should be continually asking: "Can you live with this decision? Are you prepared to face any consequences that may result?" In other words: "Is this your final answer?"

Often, just taking a few extra moments to really think through a question or problem you are trying to resolve can make all the difference in the world. Give yourself this advantage. Don't rush into decisions before carefully scrutinizing all of the ramifications and alternatives that might be available. And, finally, take advantage of all of the lifelines you have. Remember that you are not limited to three. You can use as many as you want.

In summary, make your final answers the best ones you possibly can. You might not win an instant fortune, but you can feel like a million about yourself.

Ultimately, your final answers in life should be based on which of the following?

A. *What you truly want to do*

B. *Pressure from others*

C. *Being rushed*

D. *Gambling*

The correct answer is A.

Scoring

Count up the number of questions you answered correctly throughout this article. If you answered all of the questions correctly, you are definitely worth a million at work. If you scored fifteen or more correct, you are well on your way to being worth a million. A score between ten and fourteen may mean that you need a little more help on the big money questions. And a score of nine or less indicates that you may want to reconsider your lifelines; they appear to be giving you bad advice!

Good luck and keep on growing your value, both at work and to yourself.

Peter R. Garber *is manager of Affirmative Action for PPG Industries, Inc., in Pittsburgh, Pennsylvania. He is the author of five management books, including his most recent work,* Turbulent Change: Every Working Person's Survival Guide, *and is a regular contributor of experiential learning activities and instruments to the* Annuals.

LOOK WHO'S TALKING!
THE POWER OF NONVERBAL COMMUNICATION

Judith A. Colbert

Abstract: The power of nonverbal communication has long been recognized, and communicators can obtain important information by observing the body language of their audiences. Thus, communicators of all kinds, including managers, must be aware of a full range of verbal and nonverbal cues that can help them to inspire others to function more effectively.

The author describes communication as a complex process involving the simultaneous exchange of many messages. Her thesis is that sending a message is a three-step process that includes (1) targeting the audience, (2) taking steps to make the audience receptive to the message, and then (3) tailoring the message to meet the needs of the audience.

$\mathbf{M}$ost of the time it is not enough to simply *hear* what someone is saying; we have to look at the speaker to *see* as well. The body language of our partner in communication, our "audience," can tell us what we need to say—and do—to achieve our communication goals.*

In workplace situations, managers who understand the power of nonverbal communication are better able to focus on others during the communication process. They are sensitive to nonverbal cues and are able to take steps to adjust their own communications based on the behavior they observe.

BODY LANGUAGE THROUGH TIME

The idea that body language—a popular term for nonverbal communication—is important is not new. Its characteristics and origins, in both individuals and the human species in general, have been studied by researchers working in diverse fields, including anthropology, linguistics, biology, psychology, and neuroscience.

Artists and poets have long tapped its power to convey truths. Four hundred years ago, one of Shakespeare's characters confirmed the true wantonness of a lady of questionable reputation, in spite of her verbal claims, by observing that "there's language in her eye, her cheek, her lip,/Nay, her foot speaks. . . . " Later, he praised a "true knight," who spoke "in deeds" but was "deedless in his tongue."

Modern researchers are less poetic, but they convey the same message. According to psychologist Albert Mehrabian, 93 percent of our communication is nonverbal (Center for Nonverbal Studies, 2002). That leaves a mere 7 percent for the actual words we choose. [Show Transparency #1.] Nonverbal communication is very powerful. Recent brain research has shown that we process nonverbal cues in ancient centers of the brain beneath newer speech areas. Scientific findings are helping to explain what Shakespeare and others sensed: When we have a choice, we believe what we see more readily than we believe the words we hear.

Note: Included at the end of this article are numerous exhibits that can be used as transparency or handout masters if you are presenting this material as a lecture or as part of a training session.

[Transparency #2 can be used here as a prompt for a discussion about the definition of nonverbal communication. Transparency #3 can be used as a prompt for a discussion about the elements of nonverbal communication. Transparency #4 provides some possible responses for the elements in Transparency #3.]

FACTS ABOUT NONVERBAL COMMUNICATION

Why is learning more about nonverbal communication so important? First, communication is the basis of all human interaction. Second, *effective* communication underlies successful interpersonal relationships and productivity in the workplace. Third, we can learn to improve our communication skills. Certainly, it is important to pay attention to the oral and written language skills that help us give better speeches or write more effective reports. However, given its importance, we should be directing a much greater percentage of our attention to understanding and improving our nonverbal skills.

NONVERBAL COMMUNICATION IN A MULTICULTURAL ENVIRONMENT

Another important reason to focus on the nonverbal elements of communication is the fact that the labor force contains growing numbers of newcomers from other cultures. The United States welcomed over nine million immigrants between 1991 and 2000 (U.S. Department of Justice, 2002). Many are struggling to live and work with only a minimal grasp of the English language. The International Adult Literacy Survey (Organization for Economic Cooperation and Development, 2000) found that 80 percent of foreign-born (second language) respondents had very low literacy skills and functioned below Level 3, which is considered the minimum desirable level for learning new job skills. Clearly, nonverbal communication makes an even greater difference under these circumstances.

A New Vocabulary

In a multicultural environment, nonverbal communication is complex, and much of it is culture-bound. It is not enough just to place more emphasis on the nonverbal elements of communication. It is also necessary to become more sensitive to cultural differences in the ways in which those elements are used. In some cases, that increased sensitivity may lead to a whole vocabulary of nonverbal cues that attach new significance to otherwise familiar gestures, facial expressions, and body positions.

Universal Meanings

With respect to vocabulary, the Center for Nonverbal Studies' online dictionary and other publications provide information about a whole range of cues, including both signals that researchers believe to be inborn and others that are learned or shaped by social experience. For example, extensions of the hand with the palm up or palm down are contrasting gestures that researchers have long studied. Worldwide, *palm-up* appears to have positive, non-aggressive connotations, while *palm-down* is associated with dominance and aggression. Both gestures can be used unconsciously and have been shown to have ancient neurological roots (Center for Nonverbal Studies, 2002).

[Transparency #5 can be used to extend this point by asking participants to provide other examples of nonverbal cues, what each means, and where each is used.]

Cultural Variations

Although palm-up and palm-down gestures seem to be recognized universally when associated with horizontal movement, people around the world have adopted variations for waving good-bye. For example, as Roger Axtell (1998) points out, Americans waving good-bye tend to move the forearm and hand back and forth with the hand up, *palm out* and wrist stiff, a gesture that in Europe means "no." In Europe, people usually wave with the arm up and extended out, but with the *palm down* and the hand moving up and down at the wrist. In Italy and Greece, people extend the arm with the *palm up* and curl all the fingers back and forth toward themselves in a gesture that Americans use to beckon someone to "come here."

A Full Range of Cues

These two seemingly simple gestures have complex significance and illustrate how easily nonverbal communication can be misunderstood. They show why it is important to be conscious of a full range of nonverbal and verbal cues one is giving off before assuming that a message is being transmitted and being understood.

The Benefits of Awareness

Greater awareness of one's body language and its role in communication is beneficial to both partners in the process. As communicators, we learn more about what we are saying with our bodies and have an opportunity to enhance our own nonverbal skills. As receivers, we become more sensitive to what others are "saying" and to the tools they are using.

Traditional Definitions

Traditional definitions of communication begin with the premise that it is a two-way exchange between a sender and receiver who each inhabit a distinctive environment (that is, each brings his or her own baggage) and deal with a variety of distractions (that is, "noise" in professional terms). It occurs within a particular channel (oral, written, physical) and uses a specific medium (paper, electronic disk, telephone, in person).

Within that context, senders are concerned with what they are communicating; receivers pay attention to what others are saying to them. Receivers providing feedback become senders, and thus the process of sending and receiving a message continues, much like the exchange of a birdie in a game of badminton. [Show Transparency #6.]

The Communication Experience

But the actual communication experience is more like multiple Ping-Pong games, where the balls simultaneously arc along crisscrossing trajectories that sometimes clash and sometimes reinforce each other. In such circumstances, participants succeed to the extent that they are able to recognize and effectively employ a wide range of communication skills.

Senders who focus on the content of their message and think only of their own perspective can easily be unaware of what they are communicating. Often, new insight into the messages we send comes only when we are able to see ourselves reflected in the feedback we receive. More effective communication often occurs only when the sender of the original message responds to feedback with an appropriate message.

KEY STRATEGIES

Focus on the Audience

A key strategy for improving communication skills is to tailor a message that meets the needs of the person or people for whom it is intended. That means assessing the audience by looking closely at all of the nonverbal cues, including elements in the environment. The point of such an assessment is to learn as much as possible about the audience and use that knowledge to tailor a message that will be communicated effectively. When it comes to audiences, one size does not fit all.

Ensure That the Audience Is Receptive

Even though a message is especially designed for its audience, communication will fail if that audience is not receptive. Therefore, it is important to ensure that the audience is receptive and to revise the message to suit the situation. Too often, senders miss barriers to communication that others express nonverbally. These barriers are likely to mean that a message either will not be heard or will be misunderstood.

STRATEGIES IN ACTION

Managers who understand and know how to use nonverbal communication skills have powerful tools for improving morale and productivity at work. They know, for example, that it is important to observe an employee or staff member closely before making a request. They recognize that people are unlikely to respond positively or, at best, will agree grudgingly when they are angry or resentful, concerned about problems at home, or struggling with a new language and unfamiliar surroundings. Some sample communication situations are described below.

Tony's Situation

Reaching out to others by attempting to "read" their nonverbal language can lead to more than a positive response. As the following meeting between "Tony" and his manager illustrates, reaching out could be the first step toward positive solutions that have benefits for both partners.

Tony adjusted his tie. Actually it was straight enough—he had just checked it a few minutes earlier. His palms were damp and left shiny marks where his hands had grasped the silk fabric. He kept his eyes on his manager's desk and, as he agreed to work one more weekend, his voice was low and flat. His manager was saying yet again that this contract was a great opportunity for the company and that if everyone pulled together and sacrificed now, it would mean their future was secure. At least that is what Tony thought he was saying. What Tony was really thinking about was his wife and the battle he knew he would have to fight at home. Last weekend, she had issued an ultimatum: No more weekend work or else! She did not seem to understand how important his paycheck was or consider who was going to pay the mortgage if he did not have a job.

Perceptive managers look for cues in the behavior of others and do what they can to respond to the language they "see." In Tony's case, the manager might have seen him adjusting his tie and noticed its shiny spots. He might have wondered why Tony avoided eye contact and detected reluctance in his tone of voice. Instead of remaining focused on his immediate goal and the long-term success of the company, the manager might have noticed Tony's discomfort and, at the least, acknowledged that Tony felt torn between work and family responsibilities. More positively, he might have questioned Tony further. For his part, Tony might have come to see his manager's needs from a different perspective. Together, they might have achieved a compromise, such as Tony working extra hours on one day of the weekend and being home on the other, or working overtime through the week, instead of on the weekend.

Demeke's Situation

Often assigning meaning to nonverbal cues requires sensitivity to cultural differences and an ability to move beyond familiar interpretations. Demeke's situation shows that newcomers often despair when familiar behavior and values are challenged in their new society.

Demeke had come from Ethiopia less than a year ago. He was glad to have his job, but he was not sure how long he would be able to keep it—or if he wanted to keep it. Making telephone calls was the worst of his tasks. He began by making notes, writing down everything he could think of that he might have to say. Sometimes he made a list of the people he had to call, then took it home and made his notes at night. Talking to his boss was another problem. Just yesterday, his boss had asked him to look at him and speak up. "Speak up, man," he had said, "I am talking to you!" He wished his boss understood how difficult that was for him. Back home it was a sign of respect to speak softly and lower the eyes while speaking to a superior. It seemed he would never learn a different way.

Demeke's boss must surely have seen his telephone notes and wondered if he were taking extra time for paperwork. He might also have wondered why Demeke did not speak up and explain his difficulties. The fact that Demeke seemed to be performing well in other respects should have alerted his boss to focus on his status as a newcomer from another culture. A more observant boss might have achieved more positive results by finding out what could be done to help Demeke feel more comfortable and function more effectively.

How Barriers Can Help

Through increasing one's sensitivity to the anger, concerns, or difficulties of others, nonverbal cues can pave the way to an acknowledgment that others have problems and lead to problem solving and new action plans that still solve the original goals of the communication.

Mary's Situation

Mary felt some satisfaction. The meeting with Amy had gone well—better than she had expected. Amy had been the front-line person on the customer service desk for several years. She was the first person clients met when they entered the building. In the beginning, people had commented on her pleasant manner. She had a broad smile and a warm, friendly greeting for everyone. Lately, however, she seemed different. She seldom smiled, and her voice had an unpleasant edge. Although she was superficially polite and said all the right words, people were getting the distinct impression that they were really not welcome. As her supervisor, Mary knew that she would have to act. But the question was how to get to the root of the change.

Mary decided to ask another employee to take over the reception desk for a while and invited Amy into her office. She had brought in coffee and, instead of staying behind her desk, invited Amy to join her in the informal sitting area in the corner of the room. As they chatted, Mary discovered that Amy had been trying to cope with a series of catastrophic events at home that had begun several months ago when her husband had lost his job. A very private person, fearful of losing her own job, Amy had kept her problems to herself and was only barely coping with her day-to-day responsibilities. Although saddened by what she heard, Mary was relieved. Now that she knew about the situation, she could take steps that would both help Amy and protect her company's reputation for customer service. As a start, she gave Amy the rest of the day off and set about making contacts in the human resources department that she hoped would lead to an employee assistance package that would help Amy get back to being an effective company employee.

Instead of provoking confrontation, nonverbal cues can serve as opportunities that can move communication forward and increase the likelihood of positive outcomes. Mary observed Amy at work and, based on what she saw, realized that simply telling Amy to improve her performance was not enough. It is unlikely that Amy would have been receptive to whatever Mary might have said. Working with the nonverbal cues she found in Amy's behavior, Mary took action. First, she created an opportunity to learn more, and later, she set about solving the problems that she discovered. The message she might have sent had she not interviewed Amy was changed dramatically by what she learned. As a result of her actions, it seems likely that with time Mary will both reach her own goals and be the instrument for improving Amy's situation at home and at work.

CONCLUSION

Nonverbal communication is a powerful tool. Statistically, it is responsible for the vast majority of human communication. In human terms, it holds the key to greater understanding and more effective behavior. [Show Transparency #7.] Its potential can be more fully realized when senders of messages recognize that communication is at least a three-step process: (1) targeting the audience, (2) taking steps to make the audience receptive to the message, and then (3) tailoring the message to meet the needs of the audience and still achieve the sender's goals for the communication.

In business and personal relationships, it pays to "look who's talking."

References

Axtell, R. (1998). *Gestures: The dos and taboos of body language around the world* (rev. ed.). New York: John Wiley & Sons.

Center for Nonverbal Studies (CNS). (2002). *The nonverbal dictionary of gestures, signs and body language cues* [On-line]. Available: http://members.aol.com/nonverbal2/center.htm

Organisation for Economic Cooperation and Development(OECD) and Statistics Canada. (2000). *Literacy in the information age: Final report of the International Adult Literacy Survey.* Paris: OECD. [On-line]. Available: www.nald.ca/nls/ials/introduc.htm

U.S. Department of Justice/Immigration and Naturalization Service (INS). (2002). *Fiscal year 2000 statistical yearbook,* Table 1 [On-line]. Available: www.ins.usdoj.gov/graphics/aboutins/statistics/IMM00yrbk/IMM2000list.htm

Judith A. Colbert, Ph.D., is an independent consultant, writer, and training specialist focusing on communication and administrative issues. She regularly conducts seminars and is the author of numerous distance education courses and other training materials. Formerly an adjunct professor of management communication at the University of Guelph in Guelph, Ontario, Canada, she is currently a member of the National Council of the National Association for Regulatory Administration, a U.S.-based organization for human service licensors.

LOOK WHO'S TALKING TRANSPARENCY #1

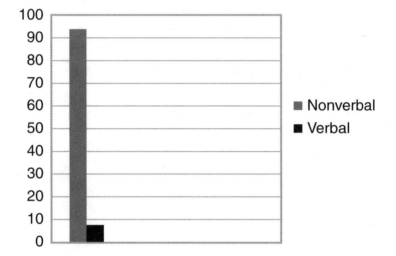

93 Percent of Communication Is Nonverbal

LOOK WHO'S TALKING TRANSPARENCY #2

What Is Nonverbal Communication?

It is the process of sending messages expressed
through elements other than words.

Other Possibilities:

Nonverbal communication is. . .

LOOK WHO'S TALKING TRANSPARENCY #3

What Are the Elements of Nonverbal Communication?			
Body	**Voice**	**Appearance**	**Location**

Look Who's Talking Transparency #4

The Elements of Nonverbal Communication			
Body	**Voice**	**Appearance**	**Location**
orientation	tone	clothing	proxemics (use
posture	speed/ pauses	accessories	of personal space)
gestures	pitch	hair	
touch	volume	skin and cosmetics	territory (immediate area
facial expressions	stammering	grooming	around a person)
and eyes	disfluences (um, er)		environment (general surroundings)

LOOK WHO'S TALKING TRANSPARENCY #5

What Do the Elements of Nonverbal Communication Mean?		
Element	**Meaning**	**Where**
palm up	nonaggressive, positive	worldwide
palm down	dominant, aggressive, may be negative	worldwide

LOOK WHO'S TALKING TRANSPARENCY #6

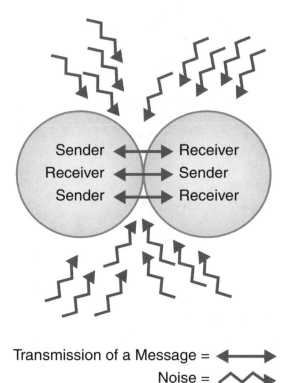

Transmission of a Message = →
Noise = ∿→

A Communication Model

Look Who's Talking Transparency #7

For Senders — Three Steps in the Process

1. Focus on the audience.

2. Take action to create a receptive audience.

3. Tailor a message that meets the needs of the audience as well as the communication goals.

COACHING FOR RESULTS:
AN OVERVIEW OF EFFECTIVE TOOLS

Marcia Ruben and Jan M. Schmuckler

Abstract: Companies see value in coaching as a leadership development tool because its effective implementation can positively impact business results. Coaching can help clients (1) become aware of their existing behaviors and habits, (2) develop new ways of working, and (3) reinforce new patterns of behavior. Appropriate tools, techniques, and practices can greatly enhance coaching effectiveness. With the increased popularity of coaching in the past decade, the number of coaching tools has increased as well. This paper describes the value of and how to use practices, tools, and assessments taken from the authors' own coaching experiences, from the initial contracting phase to the final assignment at the end of a coaching session.

Coaching has grown in popularity as a leadership development tool and so have the choices of approaches available to both external and internal corporate coaches. We strongly believe that coaches have a responsibility to familiarize themselves both with the variety of tools available and with the best time and manner to implement them. In this article we provide an overview of practices and tools that coaches can use to initiate and conduct a coaching engagement from beginning to end.

CONTRACTING (OR DO YOU REALLY WANT TO TAKE THIS ASSIGNMENT?)

The first step in coaching is contracting. Corporate coaches are typically called in through line management or the human resources department. Usually, a manager requests a coach for a direct report, although sometimes clients seek out coaching help on their own. Contracting has two steps when the request does not come directly from the client. The first is to meet with the requesting party and the second is to meet with the client. The process we follow is described below.

First Meeting with Client's Manager

During our contracting meeting with the requesting manager, we want to determine the manager's perception of the coaching "problem." We do not accept assignments unless the situation is a true developmental experience for the client and the manager actually wants the person to succeed. For example, we do not accept assignments if it becomes clear that the client's real desire is to fire the person and the company wants to be able to say that it offered coaching. The best remedy for dealing with sub-par performance is for the manager to give specific behavioral feedback and put the person on a "corrective action" path. Coaching cannot and should not substitute for this process.

The first meeting has several desired outcomes or goals:

- *Inquire about the client's willingness to be coached.* When the client is not a willing participant, his or her resistance means that the engagement cannot be successful. Coaches should be wary about taking such assignments.

- *Determine how involved the manager would like to be in the process.* Some managers want to be consulted shortly after the process begins, others halfway through, and still others just want to see results. It is our recommendation that the coach arrange for at least one session to touch base with the manager after the coaching begins. Sometimes, the client attends this meeting as well. This allows the client to ask for feedback and role clarity, which seem to be best provided with a neutral party present (the coach).

- *Determine how involved the manager is willing to be in giving ongoing feedback to the client as the coaching progresses.* Because the manager is much more likely than the coach to witness changes and/or improvements in behavior, involving the manager in giving reinforcing feedback for behavioral improvements "in the moment" adds tremendous power to the coaching process.

- *Ask for permission to share information.* Finally, we ask the manager for permission to share with the client some if not all of what has been covered in the conversation.

First Meeting with Client

In the first session with the client, coaches typically obtain a sense of the reasons for coaching. They also get a sense of the client's leadership aspirations, values, and overall goals. Coaches inquire about success factors that the client thinks are important to others, for example, to their boss, direct reports, and peers, as well as the client's perception of his or her greatest challenges. This information is helpful to the coach in determining which tools to choose from the "coaching toolkit."

Typically, the first session includes contracting on the coaching process itself. Coaches and their clients need to determine the following items:

- *Purpose of coaching.* It is important to emphasize that coaching is solely for the client's growth and development, to enhance strengths and minimize "flat spots" so that the client can be more effective. Companies typically hire coaches for their best and/or high-potential employees. Explaining this can help alleviate any resistance to coaching.

- *Length of meetings.* Our recommendation is that coaches budget one and one-half hours at least once a month for face-to-face meetings and one hour for phone meetings. Phone meetings tend to be much more focused.

- *Frequency of meetings.* How often meetings are held will vary from client to client. Generally, holding coaching meetings twice a month adds urgency and yields better results. Some corporate clients find it hard to schedule meetings that often. Therefore, it is important to convey the importance of agreeing to meet at least once a month in order to "get traction" in the coaching process.

- *How long the coaching relationship will last.* Generally, coaching relationships last a minimum of four to six months, and some can last as long as a year. The actual length depends on the nature and complexity of the coaching issues to be covered.

- *In person or by phone.* Generally, coaches give clients an option of whether to meet in person or by phone, although holding the initial session in person is usually optimal for building a trusting relationship. Coaching seems to work best when there is a mixture of both phone and in-person meetings, although some coaches work quite effectively holding all sessions over the telephone.

- *Scheduling guidelines.* Through trial and error, we have found things work most smoothly when we tell clients up-front that we have a seventy-two-hour cancellation policy and that there is a charge for cancelled meetings.

- *Process checks.* Coaches and clients agree on how they will each assess the progress of the coaching process itself and the results on an ongoing basis. A simple "What worked? What didn't work?" is often enough to keep things on track.

- *Notes and action items.* In general, we recommend that the coach send meeting notes that capture the essence of the meeting as well as agreed-on action items to the client after the session.

- *Confidentiality.* We tell clients what we will and will not share with their managers and state that we will always ask their permission before sharing *any* information. We say that general information about what we are working on may be communicated, but not the specifics. For instance, any observations about others or information about products and strategy will *not* be shared. With permission, we will share that we are working on particular skills, competencies, mindsets, and so on. Because coaching is a developmental activity and there will inevitably be both some learning and unlearning, we want to make sure that anything that is shared will not inadvertently jeopardize the client's performance evaluation.

Table 1 summarizes the key points of the contracting discussions.

Table 1. Key Points to Cover in Contracting

With Manager	With Client
• What is your perception of the coaching "problem"? • What outcomes are you seeking? • What will success look like? • Is the direct report a willing participant? • How will you communicate this conversation to your direct report? • How involved do you want to be in the coaching process? • Confidentiality	• Reasons for coaching • What are your leadership goals, aspirations? • What will success look like? • What success factors are important to your boss, direct reports, and peers? • Challenges • How often shall we meet? • How will we evaluate whether we are both on track? • Cancellation policy • Confidentiality

After the initial contracting meetings, it is time to begin the coaching process itself. The following sections describe some of the tools and practices.

ASSESSMENTS

There are numerous assessment tools available to coaches. They add value because they provide both a focus for coaching and a framework for quantifying qualitative information. Such tools should be considered as a means to extend the coach's own well-developed analytical and interpersonal skills, not as a replacement for them. The following general criteria apply to any assessment tools you may choose:

■ *Ease of use and understanding.* The tool itself should be easy to administer and not require an inordinate amount of client time. There should be a clear process for analyzing the results, as well as a presentation format that is relatively easy for the client to understand. The more clear and behavioral the feedback, the more likely that changes will take place.

- *Match to client style.* Some clients, particularly engineers, want instruments with data-driven, objective results. Others prefer more conceptual data. It is important to find out what style is the best fit for the client.

- *Match to client situation.* The most powerful feedback results are those that have a direct application to the client's current situation. Keep this in mind when choosing an instrument.

- *Validity and reliability.* Make sure there is substantial research data indicating that the instrument is valid, that is, measures what it is supposed to measure, and reliable, that is, similar results are likely to occur if the instrument is administered to the same person at another time.

- *Requirements for training or certification.* Our recommendation is that coaches receive training or certification if the publisher of the assessment requires it. Sometimes it is useful for coaches to be trained on an instrument even if it is not required so that their comfort level is high for working with the client.

The following section covers one example each of our most frequently used assessments and tools. Those include 360-degree feedback, self-assessment instruments, personality style assessments, behavioral style assessments, and specific situational assessments. (Information about obtaining the various tools can be found in the References and Resources section at the end of this article.) Also included are examples from both our own clients and from a fictional case featuring client Dave Jones.

360-Degree Feedback

The use of 360-degree feedback is focused on development rather than on assessment. The goal of the feedback is to help the client understand how his or her manager, peers, direct reports, and, sometimes, customers perceive him or her. Combining feedback from each of these groups of people creates a full circle, 360 degrees, around the client, hence, the name of the assessment tool. Such feedback can be administered via a standardized instrument or via an interview process. In either case, each group of raters is asked the same questions about the client's behavior. In a standardized version, the client generally receives a computer-generated report that summarizes results by skill area, importance, and rater group. The result is a development plan based on the feedback of the 360-degree assessment. The focus is on leveraging the identified strengths and determining an action plan for improving the critical, challenging areas.

In addition to, or sometimes instead of, a standardized instrument, coaches sometimes conduct 360-degree interviews with a set group of questions (see Exhibit 1).

- What does this person do really well? What are his or her greatest strengths?
- What could the person do better?
- How would you characterize his or her ability to articulate a clear and compelling vision?
- How is he or she at providing direction to others?
- How is he or she at giving constructive feedback?
- How is he or she at assessing performance?
- How is he or she at communicating critical information in a timely manner?
- What do you think is a blind spot the person has?
- If you had one piece of advice that could help this person to be a more effective leader, what would it be?

Exhibit 1.   Typical 360-Degree Interview Questions

Coaches ask their client to identify ten or fifteen people from whom feedback is desired and who will provide an accurate assessment of the client's behavior and skills. Coaches interview the identified group members individually either in person or by telephone. Coaches look for patterns in the data, which are then provided to the client in a synthesized report.

It is important to recognize that people tend to be defensive when receiving 360-degree feedback. This is a natural and normal reaction. The best way to deal with defensive behavior is to first let people know prior to giving them feedback that defensiveness is a typical response. For example, a couple of typical reactions are "I got this rating because of the tremendous lack of resources here" or "I don't think that it's true about me." When clients exhibit this behavior, it is best to remain calm, ask them questions, and draw them out in a way that elicits their true feelings. Another technique is to say, "What if this *were* true? Why might people be saying this?"

It is critical that the coach not only be well-grounded in the methodology and implications of the results, but more importantly, be able to help clients "connect the dots" between their greatest strengths, leadership aspirations, and the actions that will provide them the greatest opportunity for reaching their goals.

For example, consider the fictitious case of Dave Jones:

Dave was promoted to an executive vice presidential position at Standard, Inc., a struggling but still viable large cap company. Dave had been with the company for twelve years and had "grown up" there. He had done extremely well in previous positions; however, he had hit a roadblock in his current role. Although he had a great understanding of the business and was able to deliver consistent results, both peers and direct reports complained to Dave's manager that he blew up in meetings and "chewed out" people for not answering questions the way that he wanted them answered. He was sometimes curt with peers and did not inform them of critical information in a timely manner. Dave was beginning to have difficulty retaining employees. In fact, his turnover rate was the highest in the division.

To help resolve these issues, Dave's manager requested the services of a coach to work with Dave. The coach used 360-degree feedback with Dave so that he would be more aware of his direct reports' and his peers' concerns about him. It became clear during the feedback session that his interpersonal skills were an issue. Dave's strengths—his achievement orientation and drive to get results—were not tempered by an ability to motivate and develop his direct reports. He also did not listen well. Dave was able to see that all of his rater groups shared a consistent view of him. He also received strong validation for the strengths responsible for his success to date.

Whether you use a standardized instrument or one you design, the process is always voluntary and the information is confidential and anonymous. The assessment should not be tied to the client's performance review. Usually coaches wait until a person has been in a position at least six months before administering a 360-degree feedback process, because raters need enough time to get to know the person in a variety of situations so that they can provide accurate and meaningful feedback.

A coach's real value to the 360-degree process is in giving the feedback and guiding the client through a self-discovery process.

Self-Assessment

The Leadership Architect® Competency Sort Cards are often used when clients are not aware of their strengths and areas for development, when they want to know what to work on next, or when it is not feasible to do a 360-degree feedback process. Clients like the card sort because it is tangible, tactile, thorough, practical, and well-thought-out. Coaches like it because certification is not required and it is easy to use and interpret.

Coaches typically explain the origin of the cards to the client and have the client sort the sixty-seven competency cards either during a coaching session or beforehand. When the cards are sorted, the coach looks over the results, which are captured on a tally sheet. (An Excel® spreadsheet can also be used.) Coaches ask their clients whether they see any patterns or themes and also ask them whether their manager or peers would rate them the way they rated themselves. In some cases, coaches can ask the boss, direct reports, and peers to complete a card sort for purposes of comparison. The card sort can help the client become more aware of coaching goals, leadership aspirations, and competencies and also can provide a focus on the two to five behaviors that will have the greatest leverage for his or her success. Using the *Career Architect Development Planner* (Eichinger & Lombardo, 1996), *For Your Improvement* (Eichinger & Lombardo, 2000), or the *Successful Manager's Handbook* (Davis, Gebelein, Hellervik, Sheard, & Skube, 1996), coaches work with clients to choose actions that will enhance their greatest strengths and minimize the leadership behaviors that compromise their performance.

Personality Style Assessments

The Myers-Briggs Type Indicator (MBTI®) is the world's most popular and practical measure of personality dispositions and preferences. Certification is required for administering, scoring, and analyzing the instrument. The MBTI is especially helpful when a person's style or personality is the coaching challenge or when a client is having a particular problem with an employee, peer, or boss. Coaches usually tell clients that the object is to understand themselves and others better with respect to communication or problem-solving and decision-making styles. Helping clients understand their own type and then having them look at some of their employees or their manager through the lens of type can be very useful. Clients can then make appropriate adjustments to dealing with particular people or situations. Coaches are sometimes asked to do a follow-up MBTI session with the client's whole team.

For example, one client had a strong preference for the "T" (thinking) function. All her staff had high "F" (feeling) function. The staff felt as though the manager never gave them recognition. The client thought that since her direct reports were doing their jobs that they didn't need feedback. After an MBTI session with her whole team, the client gained an understanding that helped her realize that the staff needed to be recognized for doing their jobs well. Her changed behavior as a result of this knowledge allowed her to regain commitment from her staff.

> In our running example, the MBTI assessment was just what Dave Jones needed to understand the differences between his very high preference for "telling things the way they are" and others' need for a softer, gentle approach. This understanding led to a dramatic shift in his daily actions.

Behavioral Style Assessments

There are numerous behavioral style and work style assessment tools. These instruments tell clients how they and others "show up" in the world. We frequently use the Personal Profile System™ to help clients understand their behavioral profiles, learn about themselves, and identify the environment most conducive to their success. At the same time, clients can learn about the differences of others by having their team complete the profiles. Clients can understand the environment that their team requires for maximum productivity. The coach can help the client by explaining behavioral dynamics and increasing the client's knowledge of his or her unique behavioral pattern.

The Personal Profile System is not a test, and there is no pass or fail. There is no "best" profile. It is self-scoring and provides immediate feedback. There is no certification required for using the instrument; however, a thorough understanding is necessary for the coach to be effective with the instrument. Coaches must prepare by familiarizing themselves with the instrument and the scoring. The booklet contains an interpretation section and gives a few activities that coaches can assign their clients for gaining a deeper understanding of themselves. If using the instrument with a team, some team-related questions are helpful in the interpretation phase. Some examples of appropriate questions are: "What is my value to the team?" and "How can the team help me with the following developmental behaviors that I want to work on?"

> The coach used the Personal Profile System with Dave Jones. His results indicated that he was more likely to try to get things done by dominating others rather than by influencing them. The results of the Personal Profile System dovetailed with his 360-degree feedback and MBTI, and the coach was able to help him make the connections. The Personal Profile System offered Dave some clear behavioral clues for recognizing the behavioral types of those he interacted with, as well as very specific suggestions for modifying his behavior

when interacting with different types. The coach was able to observe this and give him practical feedback using Personal Profile System language as a model.

Some organizations have the executive team do a Personal Profile System feedback review together so that each team member can share his or her personal results with the rest of the team. After this event, individual results can be shared with other parts of the organization. Coaches can effectively use this executive team information with other clients in the same organization to help them improve their communication and interaction with the executives.

Specific Situation Assessments

There are some tools that are helpful for a specific behavior or situation that a client might have. For example, the Thomas-Kilmann Conflict Mode Instrument (TKI), an easy-to-administer instrument, does not require certification. The TKI booklet gives a good explanation of the conflict management grid that the coach can easily understand and teach to the client. The instrument takes ten to fifteen minutes to complete and can be administered during a coaching session. The client's profile of scores indicates the repertoire of conflict-handling skills that he or she typically uses. Coaches usually leave the booklet with their clients so that the clients can refer to the explanations in the booklet for greater understanding and for a refresher if necessary.

> For example, Dave Jones did not handle his anger very well in meetings where decisions had to be made. In order to help him understand and change his behavior, the coach chose to use the TKI, which helped Jones to understand his own actions during conflict situations that he faced.

The TKI booklet explains how certain styles are useful in specific conflicts and not as useful in others. The instrument can be used in several ways. For example, some clients use the tools with their entire team, some for conflict between two executives. Coaches need to facilitate these sessions for clients to gain the most value from the tool.

Activities and Behavioral Tools

There are a number of activities and behavioral tools that can be used with the client as part of the coaching session. These help the client focus more quickly on what he or she needs to work on and help the client practice new behaviors during the actual coaching session. One such tool is a leadership "map" and another is behavioral practices or role plays. Observation techniques are discussed here as well.

Leadership Map

Often a series of questions is used, designed to clarify the client's aspirations and goals prior to administering any other assessments. The client's answers can be used to create a "map" of his or her leadership style. As coaches go through the coaching process and clients go through the process of self-discovery, many of the questions listed below can be asked and then answered either in writing or graphically on a large piece of paper or on the client's whiteboard. This creates a word "map" or picture.

1. Imagine it is three to five years from now. What is your leadership legacy? What have you accomplished?
2. What are your greatest strengths?
3. What are your blind spots?
4. What challenges have you overcome so far? What are you most proud of?
5. What are your top three defining values?
6. What are the key relationships that you will need to nurture in order to be successful in this company?
7. What mentors do you need in order to flourish?

A leadership map is helpful because it focuses attention on high-leverage areas and therefore leads to more effective actions. Coaches review leadership maps with clients on an ongoing basis until the actions are completed. When actions are not completed, this process helps illuminate possible issues and "stuck points."

Behavioral Practice (Role Plays)

Coaches use behavioral practice when the development of new skills is required. Some clients resist the term "role play," so coaches should be sensitive to the language that they use when explaining the practice. It is important that the coach be well-grounded in management methodologies when introducing role plays. Coaches can learn effective management practices through attendance in reputable training courses. Some clients need a demonstration for role modeling, so be prepared, and be careful not to demonstrate or encourage behavior that will not lead to the intended results. For instance, saying in a demanding voice, "Get this done right away or you are fired" not only violates human resources policies, but also does not effectively motivate a worker. Finally, it is important to encourage clients to trust their own reactions to others' behaviors.

> In our example, Dave Jones was concerned about retaining a couple of his direct reports who had skills critical to the business and whose loss would have far-reaching implications. Over the course of two sessions, each dedicated to one of the people on the verge of resigning, the coach used a questioning process to ensure that Dave could really "put himself in their shoes" and understand their motivations and reactions to his behavior. The coach used the Personal Profile System model to gather information in preparing the role scripts. The coach rehearsed worst-case employee behaviors with Dave. The coach then debriefed each go-around, asking Dave to add improvements until he felt satisfied that he could comfortably handle the situation. The actual conversations went extremely well because of these focused practices in the coaching sessions.

Practicing behavior in a safe environment with a coach is a very good way to help clients build both skill and confidence. Some clients particularly like receiving instantaneous feedback and are able to make immediate improvements that are later repeated when it counts.

Observation

Observation by the coach can be a key tool for gathering information about what clients are doing or not doing well. Some venues for observation are staff meetings, meetings with clients and managers, offsite meetings with the team, all-hands meetings, and presentations.

Coaches usually set up some agreements with their clients ahead of the meeting about what will be observed and how the clients prefer to receive difficult feedback.

> In the Dave Jones example, the coach discovered that Dave's behavior in staff meetings was an issue. Dave and his coach decided that the coach would sit in on two or three meetings to observe Dave's behavior and provide feedback. Dave let his team know ahead of time that an outside person would be attending as an observer and that the observer would only be watching him. The coach sat in the back of the

room, trying to remain as inconspicuous as possible. After the first session, Dave reflected on what he thought he had done well and what could have been done differently. The coach then added additional observations. Dave made a point of incorporating some of the suggested improvements in his next meeting and asked the coach to do an informal poll among his staff on how he was doing. By the third meeting, he was more aware of his behavior and began to catch himself when he slipped back into old patterns.

Because the coach cannot always attend critical meetings, one approach is to assemble a "feedback team," consisting of the client's manager and a human resources or organization development person. In this scenario, the coach meets with the feedback team to describe what behaviors to observe and how to provide effective, consistent feedback.

Practices to Assign as Homework

The coaching process does not finish at the end of a session. In order to reinforce new behaviors or to have clients observe their own behavior, coaches should assign homework. Coaches generally call these "self-observation practices."

As coaches, we want to reinforce new behaviors and help clients achieve a level of awareness of the new behaviors. We have found that self-monitoring certain competencies or behaviors assists people in developing awareness of themselves and is more likely to result in behavioral change. Self-observation practices are especially effective for increasing awareness of influencing skills, decision-making competencies, and defensive behavior.

For example, at one high-tech firm, the client noticed that he was defensive in meetings. As a homework assignment, he was asked to observe himself and write in a journal when, with whom, and in what situations at work and at home he was defensive.

As he kept the journal, he discovered that he was not defensive at home. The behavior mainly happened in group meetings when he felt that someone challenged or attacked his new product ideas. The coachee analyzed his new awareness and realized that being questioned put him on the defensive. Because he had recently moved from Asia to the United States, the questioning in American meetings surprised him. It is not common in Asia for others to question management at a group meeting. His defensive behavior dropped significantly once he became aware of when it occurred, understood the cultural differences, and learned a couple of tips for responding to questions in meetings.

Some clients, often those in high-technology industries, don't like to keep journals, as it seems too time-consuming and conceptual. In this case, Excel spreadsheets, with which clients are already comfortable, can be used to track their awareness and behaviors as they check off the appropriate boxes on a sheet designed by the coach and the client together. Our clients have found that they can easily tally the columns to understand how much they use some of the patterns.

Coaches who are able to assign appropriate homework to motivated clients usually find that results happen more quickly. This is because awareness is always the first step toward lasting changes.

ACTION PLANNING

A key element of the coaching process is the development of a focused action plan. When clients are involved in developing their own action plans, the plans are more likely to be implemented. The process used to develop the action plan is more important than the format. An effective approach is to ask the client what type of action plans have worked in the past and what action plans have "stayed on the shelf." Based on that information, the coach and client can craft a format and process that will ensure implementation.

There are a number of formats for action plans. Typically, an action plan includes a behaviorally specific objective, specific actions to be taken to achieve that objective, names of those whose involvement is required, due dates, and results. Sometimes, a column is included to track progress by percentage of accomplishment.

> For example, in working with Dave Jones, the coach discovered that he had completed 360-degree feedback twice in his career. While talking about this subject, Dave pulled out his binder from the past and one of his untouched action plans fell out. It became clear that the traditional format had not been successful at engaging him and eliciting action.
>
> Through discussion the coach found that what had produced successful change in the past was for Dave to reflect on a challenging issue and come to what he called a "realization" about his specific behavior and why he was doing it. He was then able to develop actions based on those realizations. Upon further reflection, he realized that if he "installed" some daily, weekly, and monthly habits that

enabled these new behaviors, he would be more likely to be successful. The coach met with Dave and Dave's manager to share the action plan. The process of action planning led to significant results because of the management support and follow-up.

In the Dave Jones example, the "documentation" would look something like what is shown in Tables 2 and 3.

Table 2. Developmental Action Plan

Behavior Targeted	Realization	Actions to Change Behavior	Tips to Reinforce Behavior
Blowing up in meetings	I am expecting everyone to think and act like me.	Consciously slow down, breathe, and listen when others are talking. Do not respond unless I give a positive response.	Send meeting agenda before meeting so that staff can be more prepared. Give others more responsibility and expect them to figure out "how."

Table 3. Habits to Enable Behavioral Changes

Daily	Check my level of anxiety and take concrete steps to keep it in check, for example, by jogging.
Weekly	Hold one-on-one meetings consistently and handle challenges in those meetings.
Monthly	Ask staff for feedback on effectiveness of meetings.

Thus, the key elements of successful action planning are (1) finding out what has worked for the client in past behavioral changes and (2) adapting a plan that mirrors that success. Couple the plan with a facilitated meeting between the client and manager to make sure that new behaviors are both reinforced and recognized.

Resources for Clients

Books, articles, tapes, and executive summaries can be particularly helpful for clients who wish to increase their awareness and understanding about specific leadership skills or competencies.

Each client has a different learning style. Some clients learn best by observation, others by listening to audiotapes, others by trying new behaviors or by reading. It is important to find out the learning style of your client. You can do this by asking him or her to reflect on a time when he or she learned the most and the method of learning.

Tailoring clients' action plans to include assignments that work with their learning styles can increase their effectiveness more quickly.

> For example, the coach gave Dave Jones an article on emotional intelligence by Daniel Goleman (1998) to enhance his understanding of his interpersonal skills. Dave had indicated that he liked to read and did not have much time. Therefore, the coach assigned him an article instead of a book. After Dave completed the reading, the coach asked some focused questions about the article to increase the applicability of the article to Dave's situation.

We give bibliographies to clients and highlight books and/or articles that emphasize skill building or that increase awareness of leadership. When you have a client who likes to learn by reading, here are some steps to follow for putting together or adapting a bibliography:

- Determine the subject matter as precisely as you can by skills, competencies, or leadership/management practices. Bibliographies can be built around the following topics:
  - Influencing skills
  - Group process skills
  - Decision-making skills
  - Global/diversity skills
  - Basic management skills
  - Overall leadership processes
  - Differences between leadership and management
  - Biographies or autobiographies of great leaders

- Find titles, authors, and current status from your favorite online bookseller
- Look in reference books, such as the *Successful Managers Handbook* (Davis, Gebelein, Hellervik, Sheard, & Skube, 1996), for ideas by subject matter
- Ask colleagues for suggestions when you're stuck

In working with clients, we provide a brief summary on most frequently used books with bulleted discussion points. This summary and discussion reinforces the learnings from the books, articles, and tapes. Be sure that you have read the book or books that you recommend so that you can have a follow-up discussion. In addition, several executive book and tape services provide short summary materials or taped summaries of popular business books.

CONCLUSION

Table 4 summarizes the coaching tools covered in this article and when to use them during a coaching engagement. These tools and practices help clients focus their work on the behaviors that will provide the greatest leverage for achieving their goals and aspirations. As coaches, we need to master both our ability to listen, analyze, and summarize and our ability to choose and use appropriate tools.

Table 4. Coaching Tools Summary

Coaching Need	Tools to Use
Determine coaching focus	Leadership Map, Leadership Architect® Competency Sort Cards
Disciplined coaching process	Contracting
Awareness of strengths and developmental needs	360-degree feedback, Leadership Architect Competency Sort Cards
Development plan	Leadership Map, 360-degree feedback, Myers-Briggs® Type Indicator, Leadership Architect Competency Sort Cards
Aware of team's and/or peers' response to client	360-degree feedback

Coaching Need	Tools to Use
Conflict in styles	Interviews, Myers-Briggs Type Indicator, Personal Profile System inventories
Difficulty dealing with conflict or conflict resolution	Thomas-Kilmann Conflict Mode Instrument
Practice new skills	Role play
Change specific behaviors, for example, influence, decision making, defensiveness, assertiveness	Self-observation and journaling, observations by coach
Increase leadership competencies, for example, think more strategically, communicate more effectively, understand differences between leadership and management	Reading assignments, find internal mentor(s)

References and Resources

Audio-Tech Business Book Summaries provide both written and audiotape summaries of recent business books. They can be reached at 800–776–1910.

Biech, E. (1999). *The business of consulting: The basics and beyond.* San Francisco, CA: Jossey-Bass/Pfeiffer.

Block, P. (2000). *Flawless consulting: A guide to getting your expertise used* (2nd ed.). San Francisco, CA: Jossey-Bass/Pfeiffer.

Davis, B.L., Gebelein, S.H., Hellervik, L.W., Sheard, J.L., & Skube, C.J. (1996). *Successful managers handbook: Development suggestions for today's managers.* Minneapolis, MN: Personnel Decisions International.

Eichinger, R.W., & Lombardo, M. (1996). *The career architect development planner.* Minneapolis, MN: Lominger.

Eichinger, R.W., & Lombardo, M. (2000). *For your improvement* (3rd ed.). Minneapolis, MN: Lominger.

Eichinger, R.W., & Lombardo, M. (2001). *The leadership machine.* Minneapolis, MN: Lominger.

Goleman, D. (1998, November/December). What makes a leader? *Harvard Business Review,* pp. 92–102.

Kiersey, D. (1998). *Please understand me II: Temperament, character, intelligence.* Del Mar, CA: Prometheus Nemesis.

Kroeger, O., & Thuesen, J.M. (1988). *Type talk: The 16 personality types that determine how we live, love and work.* New York: Delta.

The Leadership Architect® Portfolio Sort Cards. These are a result of highly regarded research that focused on what made high-achieving executives successful. The research established sixty-seven leadership competencies and nineteen career "stallers" and "stoppers" that are defined behaviorally on the cards themselves. The cards can be ordered at the Lominger Limited, Inc., website: www.lominger.com.

Myers-Briggs Type Indicator. The MBTI forms and materials can be ordered through Consulting Psychologists Press, www.cpp-db.com, 800-624-1765. To qualify for ordering, one must have completed a bachelor's degree from an accredited college or university and a course in interpretation of psychological tests and measurements or an MBTI workshop given by one of several organizations. For more information, contact Consulting Psychologists Press.

Pearman, R., & Albritton, S.C. (1997). *I'm not crazy, I'm just not you.* Palo Alto, CA: Davies-Black.

Personal Profile System. The Personal Profile System is available through Inscape Publishing's authorized distributors only. For more information, contact Inscape Publishing at www.inscapepublishing.com or at 763-765-2222.

Thomas-Kilmann Conflict Mode Instrument. The TKI can also be ordered through Consulting Psychologists Press at www.cpp-db.com or 800-624-1765. No certification is required.

Marcia Ruben, principal of Ruben Consulting Group, is an organizational consultant who helps individuals, teams, and companies improve performance. Her firm focuses on organizational change management, executive development, and coaching. She has worked with leaders of Fortune 500, high-technology, and financial services companies for over twenty years. Ms. Ruben graduated Phi Beta Kappa from the University of California, Berkeley, and received her master's of science degree in counseling from California State University.

Jan M. Schmuckler, Ph.D., is an organization psychologist and leadership coach who helps executives and managers achieve goals by aligning vision, developing staff, and coaching individuals. Her expertise, drawn from twenty-five years of experience in the education, business, and nonprofit sectors, brings a unique perspective, which enables organizations to meet challenges and compete more effectively. Dr. Schmuckler holds a Ph.D. in organizational psychology from the Wright Institute, Berkeley, and B.A. and M.Ed. degrees from Temple University.

Understanding the Online Context

Heidi A. Campbell

Abstract: The Internet has created a new sphere in which to conduct business and carry on social interactions. Yet the way people utilize and view online technology has created challenges and altered the ways in which people communicate with one another. Often, businesses are so enthusiastic about becoming involved in e-commerce or implementing online communication strategies that they fail to consider the implications for their customers and workforce.

The purpose of this article is to provide background information about the Internet and highlight some of its characteristics. Several philosophical underpinnings are explored that influence how individuals relate to information and to other users in the online environment.

$\mathbf{W}$hile "surfing the net" or traveling the "information superhighway" has become a standard task for many in the workplace, the online environment is more that just a place where information and data are exchanged. The Internet and cyberspace represent a new social territory, a blending of "real" and "virtual." It is both an *information* space and a *social* space, in that people shape the information that is made available. It is best if human resources managers understand the nature of this environment before venturing online.

A Brief History of the Internet

The Internet is a global network of large computers connected via telephone lines, enabling individuals to connect with other computers all over the world. It is not a single program, but rather a collection of services and operations.

It has been said that it all began in 1957 when the launch of the Soviet spacecraft Sputnik ignited the "space race." At that time, the U.S. Department of Defense established the Advanced Research Projects Agency (ARPA), which funded diverse groups of researchers all over the United States (this eventually became ARPANET, which went online in 1969). At the time, the need for researchers to communicate with one another was considered most vital. A time-sharing system was developed at the Massachusetts Institute of Technology that enabled several individuals to interact directly with a central computer rather than waiting to submit their programs to a computer operator. This was the beginning of email. In time this system was expanded, linking computer communities across geographic boundaries. At the time programmers did not comprehend that the tools they were developing to aid their research would take on a life of their own.

Through research into thermonuclear war scenarios, Paul Baran and the RAND Corporation in California came up with "packet switching." The idea was to break data into small equal-sized packets that could travel electronically along a computer path and reassemble themselves at a given destination, eliminating the need for a central command center. This way to exchange communications was revolutionary. A hundred pages could be as easily transmitted as one line of code. Correspondence became group conversation, and mailing lists emerged as "virtual communities" (Rheingold, 1993). System engineers were kept busy redesigning the system to facilitate its increasing growth and use.

The next breakthrough in the construction of the information super-highway was the advent of the personal computer, developed at the Palo Alto Research Center (PARC). Its creators did not want to lose the highly personal communication they had grown accustomed to on ARPANET, so they developed an ethernet, a local area network (LAN) that linked all the researchers in their building. LANs allowed a great deal of information to travel quickly over short distances. At first, little distinction was made between communal and individual information.

At the time, "Internet working" was still only accessible to those inside the scientific community, but colleges and research laboratories soon gained the capabilities for networking also. Those denied access turned to newly formed networks such as CSNET and BITNET, supported by the National Science Foundation (NSF). Since networking technologies were created with government funding, "acceptable use" policies were implemented that blocked commercial activity over the networks. The question of what was acceptable use, however, was challenged by those outside wanting to get in. New networking services began to experiment with connecting individuals to supercomputers.

In the late 1980s, the High Performance Computing Act allocated funding to promote a "national superhighway for information" and to upgrade the Net for public and school access. Corporations such as IBM and AT&T began staking claims on the Net. APRANET was decommissioned in March 1990, and so began the transfer to private enterprise. In 1993 the NSF turned over the administrative function of Internet management (assigning addresses, maintaining directories and information services) to private companies, placing the Net completely in the public domain.

The original ARPANET community had numbered around a thousand people in 1969; twenty years later it numbered between five and ten million (Rheingold, 1993).

The Net formed not just a communication system, but a way of connecting people together in relationships. People became desirous of, then addicted to, and finally dependent on the communication technology. Relationships became a type of tool for dealing with technology, as well as a product of technology.

Email was a by-product of the research work done over the Internet and not the focus of the research; it was created as a way for researchers to communicate with one another. However, what began as a way to enable those separated by physical distance to contact one another quickly became one of the prime uses of the network. As this use spread to the private and business sectors, the emphasis on linking to individuals as well as finding information remained. Today email is one of the most common uses in computer networking.

PHILOSOPOHICAL ASPECTS OF ONLINE LIFE

A term often used in connection with the Internet is "cyberspace," a metaphor that emerged from science fiction literature used to describe the sphere where computer technology meets fantasy to form a new world. Cyberspace is also associated with virtual reality (VR), a human-created technological space that simulates reality and allows the user the opportunity to alter that reality in whatever ways the creator desires. It is important to note that the Internet is not just a space where data is exchanged, but a place where reality can be created and altered. Even in the business world, the philosophical idea that people are given freedom to "play God" and "create reality" cannot be overlooked, both as a powerful tool and as motivation for many computer users. Therefore, let's consider the philosophy associated with the Internet and cyberspace.

Of the many attributes that could be discussed, three stand out: (1) the Internet is situated in a simulated world; (2) on the Internet, our bodies are our words; and (3) the search for identity beyond the screen facilitates a redefined self.

A Simulated World

Cyberspace is essentially a metaphor referring to the space that is thought to exist inside a computer. Movies like *Tron* and *The Matrix* offered us a picture of this mythical space (often conceived by some computer users and marketers as an actual place). The French philosopher Baudrillard (1983) refers to this idea of simulation in his work, describing it as the "satellization of the real." He meant that when something once considered a metaphor begins to be treated as though it is part of the "real world," the idea that it is a metaphor is lost. Therefore, one must consider not just what is "real" online, but what those online conceive as being real. This is an important concept when trying to identify the boundaries and structures in online work environments.

When users refer to searching for a website through a browser as "surfing," they do not relate the action they are performing to the act of clicking a mouse that sends digits down electrical lines, contacting the computer where the information is stored and calling up the appropriate web page. Rather, the metaphor of "surfing" becomes those users' reality. Cyberspace thus becomes more than just a way of describing the space created by the networking of computers; it becomes an actual place existing in the "real" world. This perception can influence not only people's language but also how they understand the technology.

In creating a new space to function in, the simulation can become more real than the actual world. The Internet has been called a "postmodern map" for seeing and superseding the real world (Numes, 1995, p. 318). Baudrillard defines this as "third order simulacrum" (1983, p. 125) in which the "map of the territory is itself the territory." Since the commercialization of the Internet in 1993, this territory has become a public playground inhabited by a diverse population ranging from businesspeople to primary school children. One concern being voiced by pundits is how easily the lines of reality are blurred in cyberspace. The proliferation of new information technology has facilitated a blurring between what is human and what is computer. The separation or confusion of the real from the virtual has led to the discussion of disembodiment in cyberspace.

Our Bodies Are Our Words

Individuals are often known in cyberspace only by the text they produce. Many online contexts are heavily dependent on words and icons, especially email, Internet relay chat (IRC), and chat room forums. In this sense, one can say, "Our bodies are our words" online. That is, people are defined by the words they use to describe themselves. This has been called a "word-body construct," which is often flexible, composed of "information to reconstruct the meaning of the body to almost any desired depth of complexity" (Stone, 1995, p. 244).

In some circumstances, this can be difficult, as it can be hard for people to verify or authenticate their perceptions without visual cues and data. Individuals in social and work situations are often dependent on and limited by the information provided to one another online, raising the issue of whether or not people can "blindly" trust others and the information they provide.

Although images are commonly found in cyberspace, especially on the World Wide Web (WWW), until recently they typically have served only an illustrative role, often as icons providing a gateway to a section of text when they are clicked on. The technology of the Internet places emphasis on the information and on the instruments used to generate it, rather than on the individuals who actually produce it. The very nature of computer-mediated communication (CMC) focuses the user on text constructed by a specific news group or presented on a website, rather than on other human beings. The attention is on the message over the producer, the creation over the creator. Mark Numes (1995) makes the argument that, on the Internet, "Our words are our bodies," forcing us to redefine our ideas about the physical body, space, and community.

Electronic communication is essentially blind in that it erases social cues so that status, power, and prestige are not communicated (Kiesler, Siegel, & McGuire, 1984). Individuals can construct or reconstruct themselves through the information shown onscreen. This has led to many discussions of the relationship between individual identity and the computer.

Identity Beyond the Screen

Parks and Floyd (1996) said that cyberspace creates an "identity workshop." It becomes a place where people are free to experiment with different behaviors and identities because it is easier for individuals to be anonymous. Chat rooms, bulletin boards, and email allow individuals to assert various identities by using aliases or different log-in names.

The Internet is often characterized as a Utopia wherein individuals have the opportunity to re-create themselves without the bounds of social convention. For example, research has shown that individuals are less reluctant to share their personal opinions in an online discussion versus a face-to-face discussion in the workplace (Garton & Wellman, 1995; Rice, 1992; Sproull & Kiesler, 1991). The absence of social cues present in face-to-face communication (touch, facial expression, and so forth) allows group members of lower rank to participate on an equal level with those of higher status. The ability to hide one's gender, age, race, or nationality can promote equal participation.

Yet this anonymity can also lead to reduced self-regulation and uninhibited behavior. Being physically isolated from those with whom they are communicating makes some people feel less bound to social norms. The removal of social/normative constraints has been shown to contribute to extreme behavior, such as flaming (Lea, O'Shea, Fung, & Spears, 1992), the exchange of angry and often derogatory comments on a topic, usually within a discussion group. Outsiders, such as researchers or newcomers, can sometimes be subjected to flaming also. This can occur if an individual visiting or observing the group has not obtained appropriate permission to be present in the group or if he or she posts comments that are seen as "off charter."

Identity on the Internet is tied to the user's view of the world from a computer screen. Take for instance the act of logging onto another individual's personal web page. The viewer is presented with a screen of text and images, selected information chosen by its creator. Typically, there are highlighted words signaling hyperlinks to other websites or additional pages of text. The viewer can easily jump from an introduction about the individual to a commentary on favorite causes or be linked to an environmental website with a simple click. Each connection forms a link, which further separates the individual from the original person he or she sought to learn about.

Summary

In considering the philosophical underpinnings of the Internet and cyberspace, issues relating to communication and interpersonal interaction surface that have been addressed by many studies over the last decade, covering topics such as how language and metaphors are used to describe cyberspace (Benedikt, 1992), anonymity and identity online (Parks & Floyd, 1996; Turkle, 1995), and the "body" or disembodiment on the Internet (McHoul, 1997; Stone, 1992, 1995). Although only a brief overview was provided here, these ideas will have increasing importance in the future. As more and more social and business work takes place through the Internet, our methods, styles, and motivations will continue to be affected. Just as Baudrillard posits the "satellization of the real," where the metaphor become the reality, the more distanced we become from the original, the easier it will become to distort reality.

Cyberspace will continue to distance us from the basic reality of computer connections and communication lines and will continue to affect not only how we treat technology, but also how we treat other people behind the screen. Essentially, cyberspace has produced a unique laboratory to explore human interaction and communication. This "reality laboratory" not only can facilitate different methods of communication but can influence how people treat and view one another.

References

Baudrillard, J. (1983). *Simulations*. New York: Semiotext.

Benedikt, M. (1992). *Cyberspace: First steps*. Cambridge, MA: MIT Press.

Garton, L., & Wellman, B. (1995). Social impacts of electronic mail in organisations: A review of the research literature. In B. Burleson (Ed.), *Communication yearbook* (pp. 434–451). Thousand Oaks, CA: Sage.

Kiesler, S., Siegel, J., & McGuire, T. (1984). Social psychological aspects of computer-mediated communication. *American Psychologist, 39*(10).

Lea, M., O'Shea, T., Fung, P., & Spears, R. (1992). Flaming in CMC—Observations, explanations and implications. In M. Lea (Ed.), *Contexts of computer-mediated communication*. London: Wheatsheaf/Harvester.

McHoul, A. (1997, September 1). Cyberbeing and space. *Postmodern Culture, 8*(1). Available: http://muse.jhu.edu/cgibin/access.cgi?uri=/journals/postmodern_culture/v008/8.1mchoul.html&session=47875109 [last accessed June 8, 1998]

Numes, M. (1995). Jean Baudrillard in cyberspace: Internet, virtuality and postmodernity. *Style, 29*(2), 314–328.

Parks, M., & Floyd, F. (1996). Making friends in cyberspace. *Journal of Communication, 46*(1), 80–97.

Rheingold, H. (1993). *The virtual community*. New York: HarperPerennial.

Rice, R.E. (1992). Contexts of research on organizational computer-mediated communication. In M. Lea (Ed.), *Contexts of computer-mediated communication* (pp. 113–143). London: Harvester-Wheatsheaf.

Sproull, L., & Kiesler, S. (1991). Electronic group dynamics. In *Connections* (pp. 57–77). Cambridge, MA: MIT Press.

Stone, A. (1992). Will the real body please stand up?: Boundary stories about virtual cultures. In M. Benedikt (Ed.), *Cyberspace: First steps* (pp. 81–118). Cambridge, MA: MIT Press.

Stone, A. (1995). Sex and death among the disembodied: VR, cyberspace and the nature of academic discourse. In S.L. Starr (Ed.), *Culture of the Internet*. Oxford, England: Blackwell Publishers and the Sociological Review.

Turkle, S. (1995). *Life on the screen: Identity in the age of the Internet*. London: Phoenix Paperbacks.

Heidi A. Campbell earned her Ph.D. at the University of Edinburgh-Scotland in computer-mediated communications and practical theology, researching online communities and how online communication impacts interaction within a face-to-face setting. She is currently a research assistant with the Media and Theology Project at the University of Edinburgh. She is also an adjunct faculty member of the Communication Department at Spring Arbor College (Michigan). Dr. Campbell has worked as an experiential educator and has over ten years' experience as a freelance writer. Her work has appeared in publications such as Personnel Journal *and the past* Annuals. *She has presented her research at various international conferences, including the Popular Culture Association Annual Conference (USA), the British Sociological Association, and the Royal Geographic Society Annual Conference (UK).*

To Team Well or Not to Team at All? That Is the Question

Marlene Caroselli

Abstract: Despite the remarkable and measurable results of team efforts, not every organizational problem needs a team solution. Many of the small, less complicated issues that arise can be handled by a single individual or a single meeting. The questions in this article will enable potential team members to determine whether they need to form a team and, if so, how to optimize the efforts of team members.

DEFINING THE ROLE OF THE TEAM

In an interview with *Success!*, Peter Drucker (Nelson, 1995) advised business-people to focus on what the problem is instead of seeking answers. It's difficult, he said, to find answers because often the problem solver doesn't have enough data to make a decision or solve the problem. Instead, Drucker encouraged us to ask the right questions. The wrong answer to the right question, he asserted, can usually be fixed. But the right answer to the wrong question can spell disaster.

Among the most important questions teams can ask are those that help define the team and its purpose. As you read the questions below, take a pencil and circle the one(s) you feel are most relevant for your current or future team. Add any other questions you feel are necessary for your team to consider:

- What distinguishes high-performing teams from all others?
- What do the experts and the research tell us about team membership?
- Do we have those conditions?
- Who should serve on the team?
- How are teams "built"?
- What are the barriers we might face?
- What does our team need to know?
- What does our team already know?
- To what extent are team activities mission-central?
- What is our team expected to do?
- What are the boundaries within which the team will function?
- What questions will team members want to have answers for?

Having a Sponsor

Teams that have a sponsor can often do things unsponsored teams cannot. Consider these questions as you determine whether or not to team:

- Do we need a sponsor?
- What does a sponsor do for a team?
- What criteria determine the most suitable sponsor?
- What should a sponsor *not* be asked to do?
- To what extent is the sponsor involved with day-by-day team activities?
- Who's our best prospect for a sponsor?

Establishing Operational Rules and Guidelines

The metaphorical "traffic" that characterizes team operations needs traffic signs, lights, and officers. These are the ground rules that help the team maximize its work.

These questions and others will help the traffic flow:

- How are ground rules established? How are they used?
- How will voting be conducted?
- When should "outsiders" be invited to attend team meetings?
- What can be done to improve meetings continuously?
- How can feedback be used to enhance members' contributions?
- What will guide team behavior?
- What roles have to be assumed by team members?
- What negative behaviors block team performance?
- What expectations do we have for the team leader?
- What strategies foster cooperation?
- How can compromise/consensus be effected?
- What tools can be used to overcome hurdles?

- What tools are available to teams for problem solving?
- What tools are available to teams for decision making?

IMPROVING COMMUNICATION SKILLS

There's an infinite capacity, it seems, to misunderstand one another, making team communications more difficult than they have to be. By examining the following questions, you and your team can avoid some of the common communication barriers:

- What kinds of communications are we expected to produce?
- What factors should influence meeting discussions?
- How can we avoid groupthink?
- What are the sources of conflict?
- What strategies help defuse conflict?
- How can conflict be made to work for us?
- What skills do the best negotiators possess?
- When do we need to negotiate? With whom?
- What are our differences?
- How can they be celebrated so we can unite, not divide?
- Why is a team "mosaic" better than a "melting pot"?
- How can a leader bring out the best differences?
- How can we gauge the seeming impenetrability of barriers?
- How can we become unstuck?
- How can we increase our creative responses?

ENHANCING LEADERSHIP, FACILITATION, AND COACHING SKILLS

Just as the best managers know when to don and doff their leadership hats, so do the best team leaders know when to serve as facilitator and/or as coach. By studying these questions and providing possible answers, you and your team can bring out the best in one another:

- How is "team leadership" defined?
- How does the facilitator's role differ from the leader's?
- How is a team coach selected? What is he/she expected to do?
- How is "effectiveness" defined?
- What does benchmarking tell us?
- What do customers want/need/deserve?
- How can we best fulfill their expectations?
- In what sort of person do we place our trust?
- How is credibility achieved?
- How can politics work to our advantage?
- What specific techniques will help us persuade others to adopt our proposals?
- Following adoption, what can we do to ensure implementation of our proposals?
- What follow-up should occur?
- What are our next steps?

CONCLUSION

The way questions and answers are handled within an organization reveals a great deal about the corporate culture. Similarly, the way a team handles questions and answers (if they are handled at all) reveals much about the team and the members who comprise it. By exploring in advance issues such as those embedded in the questions presented above, individuals and organizations increase dramatically the likelihood of success in response to the basic issues:

- Do we need to form a team? and
- If so, how can we increase its chances for success?

Reference

Nelson, R. (1995, July/August). How to be a manager. *Success!*, pp. 66–69.

Marlene Caroselli, Ed.D., presents corporate training and keynote addresses on a variety of subjects. She also has written forty-nine books and curriculum guides to date.

LEVERAGING DIFFERENCE AND DIVERSITY IN MULTICULTURAL TEAMS, VIRTUALLY OR FACE-TO-FACE

Dianne Hofner Saphiere

Abstract: This article summarizes the findings of a nine-month study correlating global business team behavior with productivity. It offers five intervention/training methods for facilitating productivity in diverse and dispersed teams, either virtually or face-to-face. These methods center around a team working on its actual task: to integrate business and intercultural communication competencies, leverage differences as personal traits based on culture rather than as stereotypes or generalized representations, and teach team members to be both process facilitators and cultural interpreters.

In today's world pretty much any work team is multicultural. It likely includes people from different functional areas of the organization who are of different genders, ages, ethnicities, races, spiritual traditions, and sexual orientations. When a group of people has radically differing values and priorities, not to mention communication and decision-making styles, it can feel next to impossible to achieve agreement.

CORRELATING PRODUCTIVITY AND MULTI-TEAM BEHAVIOR

One key study on this topic, "Productive Behaviors of Global Business Teams," was reported in a specialized journal with limited access to general practitioners: the *International Journal of Intercultural Relations* (Hofner Saphiere, 1996). Subjects of this nine-month study were twelve global business teams: fifty-six people representing nine nationalities and eleven companies. Of the fifty-six study participants, eleven were women. The aim of the study was to determine which behaviors correlated with productivity, as rated by the team's supervisor and by the team members without allowance for environmental factors (economic downturns, for example).

Findings

Noteworthy findings included the fact that productive teams engaged in two and one-half times more task and nearly four times more process behavior than did unproductive teams. They expended more effort both on the work at hand and on teamwork and coordination. They communicated with one another 53 percent more frequently than did the less productive teams, remaining informed of team progress and sharing their perceptions of their teamwork. Significantly, productive teams placed a high value on social interaction (this value statistically correlated with productivity) and engaged in frequent informal conversation (also statistically significant). This resulted in members of productive teams feeling understood and respected; they unanimously desired to work together again—a very simple and seemingly revealing test of a team's productivity!

In contrast to the focus on team process, or perhaps a crucial element of it, productive teams expressed differences of opinion more frequently than did less productive teams. They disagreed more, both in person and in correspondence. One telling differentiation was that productive team members disagreed in a depersonalized manner 50 percent more often. They debated the validity of the *issue* at hand, not of the *person* who held the opinion. It is also worth pointing out that productive teams balanced their disagreement with many positive depersonalized statements when communicating in writing. That is to say, in email, fax, and reports, productive teams critically analyzed the task at hand and also shared encouraging comments about the team's progress.

Productive teams varied their communication according to the medium they were using and used several communication media to balance task and affect. In face-to-face meetings, they spent significant time on relationship building as well as task; they used email and written communication to maintain accuracy, for record keeping, and to build on one another's individual work; and they used teleconferences to gauge the emotion and commitment around an issue. It was interesting to observe that written communication, while highly task-focused, began and ended with relationship-building information.

Other findings indicated that productive teams rotated leadership among members and that the leader assumed a role of process facilitator, sharing his or her ideas early on to "model" that disagreement was acceptable, structuring the process so that all could contribute, and creating an atmosphere of mutual support and task orientation. Productive teams utilized a repertoire of alternative problem-solving methods, depending both on the desired outcome and the needs of the team members. The results seemed to indicate that the primary purpose of global business teams was to exchange information from diverse perspectives and come to workable, worldwide solutions—a key finding.

A final noteworthy and statistically significant finding was that productive teams took proactive responsibility for cultural mediation and interpretation—putting cultural assumptions and preferences out on the table to promote understanding and group agreement on a process that would allow team members to operate at their best. A key point here was that productive teams shared this responsibility among their membership.

Implications

A key implication from this study was that, while nationality influenced behavior, business function, international experience, and personality seemed to be just as valid predictors. Actually, many of the study participants had difficulty choosing a national classification, as many of them were so internationally bred.

Implications for trainers and facilitators were four-fold:

1. Process facilitation abilities are of crucial importance when working with multicultural teams.

2. Team facilitators must be able to counsel and motivate people regarding the advantages of diversity and of using alternative discussion and problem-solving approaches.

3. Existing intercultural interventions are too oriented to nonprofit organizations and academia. New business models that meet the expectations and realities of business must be developed.

4. A facilitator's ability to use graphics or drawings to forge common understanding and bridge language gaps is vital.

Implications for the design of training programs included:

1. Training for global business teams should be task-focused and, ideally, involve the team working on its actual business or operational needs while the facilitator teaches and develops, using a process facilitation approach.

2. Training must go beyond comparative cultures ("They do things this way in France") and equip people with the skills they need for the intercultural, multicultural dynamic. Team members need tools for understanding and leveraging differences without labeling one another according to stereotypical national, racial, or ethnic categories. Team members want to be treated as individuals, not as representatives or mouthpieces for some larger group.

3. Training in methods for accomplishing tasks and building relationships via technology, across distance and differences, is a high priority.

4. Training in methods for interpreting and mediating differences is highly needed.

A Renewed Purpose

Although I had been facilitating diverse, dispersed teams since the early 1980s, this research study brought the next steps for such work into perspective. To summarize, I decided to develop some tools and methods to enable diverse, dispersed work teams to do the following:

1. Pay more attention and put more effort into both task and process/relationships.

2. Gain the benefits of social interaction (knowing and trusting one another) more quickly, via the task and via technology.

3. Learn the value of expressing different opinions and some methods for doing so constructively.

4. Develop each team member as a process facilitator and a cultural interpreter/mediator.

5. Learn about one another in deep and meaningful ways that make a difference to team functioning and task accomplishment—without labeling or stereotyping.

6. Do their work (focus on task) while they learn and improve their intercultural communication skills.

7. Develop skills for the intercultural dynamic, using comparative cultural information as background or a jumping-off point and dialoging with team members to create team cultures that work.

8. Better integrate business skills and intercultural competencies so they are not separate learnings.

The following five methods, along with their tools/worksheets at the end of this article, were the result.

Method 1: Skills for Decision Making Across Differences

One method for accomplishing these objectives is to use five handouts describing communication skills ("Paraphrasing/Building Common Ground," "Clarifying and Sharing Mental Models," "Developing a Comprehensive Picture/Mutual Learning," "Creating Solutions," and "Maintaining Objectivity and Open Mindedness") as a basis of discussion during a virtual or face-to-face team meeting. (These handouts are provided on pages 246 through 255.)

The skills selected integrate business and intercultural competencies into one skill set. The lists include skills that seem quite simple and perhaps even common sense. However, like listening skills, they are skills for which most of us can use more practice.

Goals

- To develop intercultural business skills while working on task.
- To refine team culture and ground rules to best use all team members' expertise.
- To improve team members' abilities to act as process effectiveness consultants for their own team.

Process

1. Prior to a team task meeting, do a short "lecturette" on one of the skill lists to ensure all team members understand the meaning of those skills.

2. Explain that as the team works that day, you want them to make special efforts to use the skills on the list. They don't have to agree with the skills or like them, but for the session that day they will use them and see what happens.

3. As the team members work on their task, encourage them to structure their discussion so that they practice the skills from the handout. (*Note:* When first beginning work of this type with a team, prepare process ideas ahead of time. For example, with "Paraphrasing/Building Common Ground," there might be a rule that for the first forty minutes every statement must be paraphrased at least once by another person before a second thought can be introduced. Of course, this will slow down the process, but it will usually add greatly to the meaning and reveal misunderstandings.)

4. At periodic intervals, check to make sure/encourage team members to pay attention to the skills they are to practice.

5. Once a specific activity is finished, ask team members what they noticed about using the skill/process. Ask what its advantages as well as its disadvantages were. The team may agree that it wants to continue using one of the skills on the list, and it would then add this to its team ground rules/communication guidelines.

6. After the meeting, invite reflection and discussion of both task and process.

7. Use another skills list for the next team meeting, building on prior skills.

8. Continue to refine the team's ground rules by using the "Our Commitment" sheet on page 256 at the end of this article. It will help the team make decisions in the future and remind them of how they said they wanted to communicate with one another. On the worksheet, "off-limits" indicates words and phrases the group feels are "loaded" and that they agree to avoid using. "Red flags" are behaviors the group judges to be indicative of an inappropriate process. For example, "repetition of an idea" might be on a team's red flag list. When a team member says the same thing several times, a colleague may make some previously agreed-on gesture to indicate the repetition. The group then knows to stop the discussion to determine the cause of the repetition. If someone feels that he or she hasn't been heard and acknowledged, the group deals with the issue before proceeding with the task.

METHOD 2: INDIVIDUAL STYLES

This method is best utilized early in a team's development, although it can be revealing at any stage.

Goals

- To promote mutual understanding of one's self and other team members.

- To refine team culture and ground rules to best use all team members' expertise.

- To accomplish a task more quickly and synergistically.

Process

1. Distribute the sheet titled "Individual Styles—Components of Team Effectiveness" (page 257) to all team members and ask them to complete it.

2. Share the results with all team members in a manner appropriate to the team. This might mean starting every face-to-face or virtual meeting with each team member sharing just one component, or with team members taking turns discussing a column/category of interaction that seems to be

causing problems in communication (row three) or disagreement (row five), for example.

3. Encourage the team to revisit its ground rules ("Our Commitment") and add to, edit, and delete as appropriate based on any new information. The goal should be to leverage the input and expertise of each team member and make contributing effectively as easy and comfortable as possible.

METHOD 3: ANALYSIS OF TEAM MEMBERSHIP AND TASK EFFECTIVENESS

This method can be used after Method 2 above, or it can be used on its own.

Goals

- To recognize that diversity is an asset to task accomplishment.
- To refine team culture and ground rules to best use all team members' expertise.

Process

1. Distribute the worksheet "Analysis of Team Membership and Task Effectiveness" on page 258 to all team members and ask them to complete it.

2. Discuss everyone's answers and generate a group summary that captures the key points.

3. Come to group agreement about the "how to use," "what to avoid," and "how to compensate" portions of the sheet, incorporating the information as appropriate into the team ground rules on the "Our Commitment" sheet.

METHOD 4: "SHOW AND TELL" MUTUAL LEARNING EXERCISE

This method is best used when there is a merger of two or more organizations or divisions and, thus, of two or more corporate cultures.

Goals

- To develop shared understanding of the strengths and improvement areas of each organization.

- To reduce the anxiety involved in a merger by allowing people to state what's important to them and their fears regarding what might be lost.

- To develop agreement on what the merged organization will look like, its major components, and roles of the key players/corporate cultures.

Process

1. Distribute the sheet "'Show and Tell' Mutual Learning Exercise" from page 259 to all team members and ask them to complete it.

2. Encourage team members from each company or division to reach consensus prior to a joint meeting.

3. During the face-to-face or virtual meeting, each group presents to the other group. The listening group is encouraged to ask clarifying questions and to summarize to the satisfaction of the presenters.

4. The group should summarize what it wants to maintain and to avoid in the merged organization, its ideas for structuring the merged organization, and processes for doing the work.

METHOD 5: STAND IN THE OTHER'S SHOES

This method is best used when there are rivalries or animosities on a team. It's a partner activity and works well when team members who most dislike or apparently misunderstand each other are paired.

Goals

- To foster shared understanding, empathy, and respect among team members.

- To refine team culture and ground rules to best use all team members' expertise.

Process

1. Distribute the worksheet "Stand in the Other's Shoes" from page 261 to all team members. Assign partners and ask them to complete their worksheets.

2. Team members should take turns speaking as their partner—reporting to the group as if they were their partners.

3. They must obtain the agreement and satisfaction of their partners for their answers to each question. Partners are allowed to dialogue until the reporter is able to answer the question to the satisfaction of the listening partner.

4. After partners have successfully reported, ask team members how the experience felt to them and whether they achieved any insight (usually rivals know each other very well, even though they think they do not).

5. Encourage the team to reflect on its ground rules and change, edit, add, or delete as appropriate based on their new learning.

CONCLUSION

It is my hope that the methods suggested in this article will in some small way help practitioners to better enable diverse and dispersed work teams to leverage difference and diversity in their decision making. Key issues to consider are fourfold:

1. How to encourage a team to work on its business task while improving its processes and members' skills.

2. How to better integrate business and intercultural communication competencies into training and development.

3. How to deal with differences as personal traits based on national and ethnic culture as well as on personality, family background, education, training, and so forth.

4. How to encourage a team's independent competence by enabling team members to serve as effective process facilitators and cultural interpreters.

References

Bartlett, C.A., & Ghoshal, S. (1989). *Managing across borders: The transnational solution.* Boston: Harvard Business School Press.

Carmel, E. (1999). *Global software teams: Collaborating across borders and time zones.* Upper Saddle River, NJ: Prentice Hall.

Elashmawi, F., & Harris, P.R. (1998). *Multicultural management 2000: Essential cultural insights for global business success.* Houston, TX: Gulf.

Funakawa, A. (1997). *Transcultural management: A new approach for global organizations.* San Francisco, CA: Jossey-Bass.

Hampden-Turner, C., & Trompenaars, F. (2000). *Building cross-cultural competence: How to create wealth from conflicting values.* New Haven, CT: Yale University Press.

Hofner Saphiere, D. (1996). Productive behaviors of global business teams. *International Journal of Intercultural Relations, 20*(2), 227–259.

Hofner Saphiere, D. (2001). *Redundancía: A foreign language simulation.* Leawood, KS: Nipporica Associates.

Hofner Saphiere, D., & Nipporica Associates. (1997). *Ecotonos: A multicultural problem-solving simulation* (2nd ed.). Yarmouth, ME: Intercultural Press.

Hofstede, G. (2001). *Culture's consequences: Comparing values, behaviors, institutions and organizations across nations* (2nd ed.). Newbury Park, CA: Sage.

Marquardt, M., & Horvath, L. (2001). *Global teams: How top multinationals span boundaries and cultures with high-speed teamwork.* Palo Alto, CA: Davies-Black.

O'Hara-Devereaux, M., & Johansen, R. (1994). *Global work: Bridging distance, culture and time.* San Francisco, CA: Jossey-Bass.

Rosen, R., Digh, P., Singer, M., & Phillips, C. (2000). *Global competencies: Lessons on business leadership and national cultures.* New York: RHR Enterprises.

Seelye, H.N., & Seelye-James, A. (1995). *Culture clash: Managing in a multicultural world.* Lincolnwood, IL: NTC Business Books.

Trompenaars, F., & Hampden-Turner, C. (1997). *Riding the waves of culture: Understanding diversity in global business* (2nd ed.). New York: McGraw-Hill.

Dianne Hofner Saphiere *has facilitated intercultural effectiveness for some of the world's largest firms since 1979. She has lived in four countries and worked with people from forty-five. A frequent author, online moderator, owner of Nipporica Associates, and a founder of CultureWares, Ms. Hofner Saphiere has been on the faculty of the Summer Institute for Intercultural Communication since 1990. In 1994 she received the Interculturalist Award of Achievement from the International Society for Intercultural Education, Training, and Research.*

Skills for Decision Making Across Difference: Paraphrasing/Building Common Ground

1. Be sure to check your understanding frequently.

   - We are human and we tend to listen with filters on—through our biases and perceptions. Step back, be aware of your own colored glasses, and share what you have heard so the speaker can correct you.

2. State what you have heard using words different from those of the speaker.

   - We can hear things twice and three times and still mishear. We define words differently. We hear what we want to hear or are afraid of hearing. Restating what we have heard using our own words allows us to connect what the speaker intended to say and what we actually heard.

   - Don't be afraid to learn something new. We may have to unlearn our preconceptions in order to "hear" the real story.

   - While clarity is key to mutual understanding, asking people to clarify their comments or repeat themselves in a tense or delicate situation can have dangerous side effects. It can appear that you are doubting, attacking, disbelieving, or attempting to gain time to form your rebuttal.

3. Put yourself in the speaker's shoes to clarify; use words and phrasing with which the speaker can feel comfortable.

   - Reversing roles forces us to listen; it prevents us from jumping ahead, forming our own thoughts, or preparing a defense or debate.

   - Speaking in a manner that makes the speaker comfortable helps the speaker feel understood and is a wonderful method for building mutual understanding, empathy, and trust.

4. The speaker is judge.

   - The person whose comments we are clarifying must feel satisfied that we have understood.

5. Look for both commonalties and differences in order to build common ground; both are needed.

   - Verbalize what you see members of the group sharing, as well as ways in which members are different. This provides an additional check for misunderstanding.

   - Attempt to relate differences and commonalties to team objectives.

6. Emotions are as important as content and task.

- People create, manage, and work in organizations. People make businesses successful and can cause them to fail. And people have feelings.

- Feelings aren't "right" or "wrong"; they are real, they exist, and they need to be dealt with.

Skills for Decision Making Across Difference: Clarifying and Sharing Mental Models

1. Be supportive; affirm others' opinions and experiences.

   - Remember that people do the best they can under the circumstances. In their context, with their experience, they are "right."

   - Verbally and nonverbally supporting other team members will encourage them to share more information, thus leading to a more complete decision.

2. Understand more deeply than you think you need to.

   - We may not realize how little we know; we need to explore others' thinking. Mutual understanding has a way of naturally overcoming resistance and producing agreement. When you think you've understood, check your understanding one more time.

   - Ask questions to learn how the speaker's thinking applies in different situations.

   - Probe the past, present, and future of the issue under discussion.

3. Make sure everyone on the team understands.

   - Ask several different people to summarize at each juncture.

   - Check team members' facial expressions and nonverbal communication for possible misunderstanding, disagreement, wandering minds, and so on.

   - Frame "learning mode" and "information gathering" as the most open, productive, confident, and effective methods of operation over the long term.

4. Make sure everyone understands the same thing.

   - Draw pictures, charts, or diagrams, make analogies, or take group minutes or notes. Use different methods to ensure that understanding is shared.

   - Include people unfamiliar with your topic at key intervals in your discussion. Someone not so involved with the issues can ask the naïve questions that those familiar with the issue may not think of.

   - Link what you hear to the team's objectives. The core essence of apparently disparate ideas may contain much commonality.

The 2003 Annual: Volume 2, Consulting/© 2003 John Wiley & Sons, Inc.

5. Clearly demarcate all transitions and decisions, even the most minor.

- Prior to or at the beginning of a meeting, create an agenda and stick to it. Clearly and frequently indicate to all team members where the group is.

- Explicitly verbalize movement of discussion from one topic to another.

- Clarify and summarize currently perceived choices, priorities, concerns, and reasoning for all team members.

- Identify unresolved issues.

- Use an unbiased third party as facilitator when necessary.

SKILLS FOR DECISION MAKING ACROSS DIFFERENCE: DEVELOPING A COMPREHENSIVE PICTURE/MUTUAL LEARNING

1. Speak clearly.

   - Use short, clear statements; speak precisely and reduce inconsistency.

   - Pause to allow for comprehension and questions.

   - Don't assume that others understand; clearly explain your intentions, purposes, and rationale.

   - Speak your own truth for yourself; don't project onto others.

   - Express feelings honestly and without blame.

2. Listen actively.

   - Demonstrate your attentiveness by asking questions, giving feedback, and using encouraging nonverbal communication.

   - Listen for subtle differences, then clarify and summarize.

   - Listen in many modes: formally and informally, one-to-one and in groups, verbally and nonverbally, explicitly and implicitly, intuitively and rationally.

3. Establish a safe learning environment; be curious.

   - Acknowledge and validate others' experiences and opinions.

   - Choose and practice an appropriate communication style (candor, reassurance, openness, and so on) to put others at ease.

   - Always assume you need to know more; the best decisions frequently emerge from a complete picture.

4. Shift perspectives; sort and synthesize information.

   - Group or arrange information in order to obtain more information and a more complete picture. Integrate diverse pieces of information into an overall whole through methods such as mind mapping, affinity diagramming, or categorizing. Remember to focus on overall objectives.

   - Address the issue in different ways. For example, if you're talking about systems, shift to examining how that information would affect structure. If addressing cognitive aspects of an issue, switch to include feelings as well; if analyzing, intuit as well.

- Consult multiple sources—all levels and functions—and all parties even peripherally concerned (they may be more involved than you think).

5. Plan ahead when possible.

- Plan when, where, and how the communication will take place; structure and forethought tend to result in more group learning.

- Prepare for potential problem areas and plan how to manage for win-win solutions.

SKILLS FOR DECISION MAKING ACROSS DIFFERENCE: CREATING SOLUTIONS

1. Agree to disagree; conflict can be positive.

   - Although it's easier to reach agreement if people are under the sway of groupthink, differing opinions and perspectives are obviously wiser over the long haul. We need to cultivate good working relationships with people we disagree with so that we can learn from them. Conflict can cause us to examine the situation more thoroughly, providing us with different perspectives.

2. Don't limit yourself to either/or choices.

   - If we limit ourselves to only a few possibilities, we may overlook the best solution. Our strategy should not require us to give in or "compromise," nor to demand that of others. Solutions should incorporate as many of the positives as possible, while minimizing the negatives. We should be in analog mode, generating new solutions, not digitally limiting ourselves to a choice between positions.

3. Be aware of differences.

   - Most people underestimate differences. It is impossible to build a relationship or come to a mutually acceptable agreement based on the belief that we are right and that others are somehow unenlightened. It is nearly always possible to achieve a depth of understanding at which we have common objectives and desired outcomes. Be inclusive thinkers.

4. Don't make behavior contingent or dependent.

   - Don't count "favors" or wait for the other person to go first. Each of us must proactively act for the common good, knowing that it is the best way to engender trust. Be trustworthy.

5. Don't choose sides.

   - Avoid stereotypes and prejudgment; premature commitment or predetermined solutions may derail agreement. We need to remain open to revising our views as we obtain more information.

   - Maintain openness to alternatives; having too many "set" attitudes works against us. Listen, understand, and explain; don't attempt to persuade, influence, or negotiate.

6. Always consult before deciding (ACBD).

- Involving people in a process of making decisions and generating solutions will provide more accurate and complete information and ensure buy-in and implementation.

- Consulting with others produces a more informed decision, promotes better understanding, encourages two-way communication, helps to balance emotion with reason, avoids the appearance and reality of coercion, and establishes a mutually productive and trusting working relationship.

SKILLS FOR DECISION MAKING ACROSS DIFFERENCE: MAINTAINING OBJECTIVITY AND OPEN-MINDEDNESS

1. Focus on your purpose.

   - Remember that you are attempting to find the best solution for the business and for all concerned.

   - Explore mutual interest; don't focus on predetermined positions.

   - Have your team reiterate its purpose frequently, using as many different methods as possible.

2. Take care of yourself (your body, heart, and mind).

   - Breathe deeply. Lean back, stand up, stretch, or take a break. Exercise your smile muscles. Tell the group a joke, or just think of something funny. Listen to some music. Move.

   - Take a mini vacation.

   - Make conscious and committed efforts to include fun in your life during stressful times: laughter, noncompetitive play, time with children, a mental joy list.

3. Maintain a creative environment.

   - Use all your senses. Put things in your workspace to remind you to lighten up and see the creative possibilities (posters, pictures, and toys).

   - Pursue a sense of adventurousness: Go along for the ride and see where you end up rather than worrying about not having control.

   - Seek an innocent mental outlook: Remember all the basic questions and fresh ideas you had when you were new to your job or the organization? Try to recapture that creativity, sense of wonder, and possibility.

   - Focus on the positives facing the group, what you already know, what is not broken. We choose to define the challenge we are facing: opportunity or crisis; chance to learn and do new things or to feel overwhelmed and out of control.

   - Engage in positive rituals at key junctures to bring the group together and reinforce a sense of progress.

4. Keep things fresh. Vary approaches, leadership, and perspectives.

   - Talk to people outside the organization, outside your field, and unrelated to the project at hand—your uncle, the butcher, the baker, or the

candlestick maker may be able to provide you fresh outlooks and help
you keep things in perspective.

- Go from macro to micro and from examples to visions.

- Use mind maps, drawings, physical movement, analogies—anything
other than just lists or head-to-head debates. Don't get stuck in a rut.

- Practice thinking in another's shoes/advocating from a perspective
other than your own. This will bring you fresh ideas and insights.

5. Deal with fear; don't ignore it.

- Make the time and space to let yourself feel what you are feeling.
Emotions are real and will not just go away; they may erupt at inop-
portune moments if you remain unaware they are there.

- Determine the origins of your fear: Fear of losing what you have?
Fear of the unknown? Once you've labeled the fear, you can imagine
worst-case scenarios and contingency plans, improving your ability to
make the most out of any situation.

- Take yourself lightly and the challenge seriously. Consciously integrate
humor into the process.

Our Commitment

Decision-Making Process

Communication Skills

Off-Limits

Red Flags

The 2003 Annual: Volume 2, Consulting/© 2003 John Wiley & Sons, Inc.

Individual Styles — Components of Team Effectiveness

The strength of a team is that its members can more thoroughly analyze the relevant factors involved in a decision from diverse viewpoints. Team members also bring a variety of communication, decision-making, and conflict-resolution skills to the table, which, when blended well together, improve a team's overall effectiveness.

Describe your preferred style:	On a team, when do you feel most productive, like you're contributing your best?	When do you feel most ineffective, misunderstood, frustrated, or powerless?	In what type of situation is your preferred style most useful?	How can your style be negatively perceived/ when is it a disadvantage?
When communicating with cross-functional peers (making a point, understanding others).				
When participating in an important decision-making process.				
When faced with direct disagreement or conflict among team members.				

ANALYSIS OF TEAM MEMBERSHIP AND TASK EFFECTIVENESS

1. Given the objectives of this team, describe some of the tasks that you as a team are going to need to be able to accomplish and the styles/approaches most useful to accomplish them.

Task	Style Needed	When/Why

2. List the styles your team has and how you as a team can best ensure that the styles are used at appropriate times.

Style	How to Use	What to Avoid

3. List the styles your team is missing and how you as a team can best compensate.

Style	How to Compensate	What to Avoid

"Show and Tell" Mutual Learning Exercise

Instructions: The purpose of this exercise is to ensure that all team members understand the work of both organizations, how each is structured, how the work is accomplished, and the strengths and areas for improvement of each organization from the perspective of that organization.

This is your opportunity to explain yourself so that the crucial elements of your business are maintained and optimized/improved on in a merged organization. The goal is to improve business effectiveness and customer satisfaction. You will be expected to be as honest, articulate, concise (brief), and objective about your current business as possible.

Spend individual time answering/thinking about the four questions below. Prior to the meeting, meet with other team members from your organization to prepare a fifteen-minute presentation to team members from the other organization on one flip chart or PowerPoint slide.

Questions to Consider

1. What are the key contributions your organization makes to the business—those things that must be accomplished in order for the business to be successful?

   - Some key tasks your organization must perform:

   - How the tasks are best accomplished:

2. What are the current strengths of your organization—things your organization is proud of and worked hard to make happen—that you'd like to see preserved in a merged organization? (Include skills and expertise, processes, flow, systems, management techniques, and so forth.)

- What are these strengths?

- Why are they important to the business?

3. What are the biggest areas for improvement in your organization that would help you more effectively contribute to the success of the overall business? (Include inefficiencies, systems, processes, hand-offs to others, structure, skills, expertise, management, and so on.)

- Explain the issue and why it's an issue.

- Give some ideas on how it *should* be or elements an improved situation would contain.

4. From your organization's perspective, how does it feel to enter this merger process?

STAND IN THE OTHER'S SHOES

Instructions: The purpose of this exercise is to be able to put yourself in the shoes of a fellow team member—to practice getting outside yourself and to perceive the world from another perspective.

We realize that not all of you know one another that well, and that there is going to be a significant amount of guesswork. Your objective is *not* to tell us how your fellow team member is perceived, but to give yourself the experience of *being* your fellow team member.

Think about the team member you have been assigned. Think about his/her experience, background, education, function, position, style, gender, age, personality, and so forth.

You are:

1. How would you describe yourself?

2. What most motivates you—what gets you excited and keeps you going?

3. What types of situations are most frustrating for you?

4. What contributions do you see yourself able to make to this team?

5. When working on an important task, what causes you to become "stuck"?

FUTURE AREAS BECKONING PARTNERSHIPS BETWEEN HUMAN RESOURCE PROFESSIONALS AND INDUSTRIAL/ORGANIZATIONAL PSYCHOLOGISTS

Robert T. Brill

Abstract: Industrial/organizational (IO) psychology is an important discipline grounded in rigorous scientific investigation of psychological phenomena in the workplace. The author posits that IO psychologists and human resource professionals must make a commitment to a more mutually supportive relationship in order to be more effective at coping with the challenges posed by the swiftly changing workplace. The author explains why the scientist-practitioner distinction should be deliberately avoided and replaced with greater overlap in which both disciplines share in the development of critical theoretical models and essential data collection, as well as the development and implementation of effective work interventions.

A discussion of the nature of these partnership roles is followed by an overview of three specific areas of interest in which such collaborative efforts will be greatly needed. Issues related to selection, training, and the psychological contract between employer and employee are discussed.

The world of work is riding a wave of explosive new variables when understanding, predicting, and managing the psychology of the workplace. Human resource (HR) professionals are currently immersed in uncertain waters, working to rise above the crest with proactive and reactive coping strategies. Industrial/organizational (IO) psychologists will continue to help in this endeavor by providing insight and applications for more healthy and productive workforces.

Industrial/organizational psychology involves "the development and application of psychological theory and methodology to problems of organizations and problems of individuals and groups in organizational settings," according to the American Psychological Association (1981, p. 666). In my opinion, there has thus far been a less than optimal functional relationship between theorist/researchers and practitioners in the business context. The mutual support between disciplines has been underutilized, and that greater synergy in the HR-IO psychology relationship will be important for the imminent HR transformation (Minehan, 1998) and for international businesses to survive and thrive in the global village.

Industrial/organizational psychologists should begin to focus on ways to better serve the specific needs of the HR professional per se. May (1998) reiterates this beckoning partnership:

> "It is clearly time for a quantum leap in the HR field, and IO psychologists working with and for HR professionals can support this transition by taking seriously the organizational pressures to change, helping to identify ways to measure the value delivered by HR, and conducting meaningful research related to all areas of human performance in tomorrow's organizations." (p. 31)

The factors that have constrained or limited the relationship between the two disciplines (need for research control versus sensitivity of information exchange; emphasis on understanding and confirmation versus business priorities and utility focus) may never be fully extinguished. However, a more concerted effort to unite the talents and assets of the groups is mandated by the drastic changes taking place in the workplace. Business, society, and especially individuals could drown in the complexity with which they are confronted (Guterman, 1994) due to globalization, surges of technology, rapidly shifting cultural dynamics, and the glut of available information, to name a few pertinent issues (Howard, 1995). Consequently, four types of partnership objectives that HR professionals and IO psychologists will need to pursue in order to handle the future challenges of revitalizing the human resource are discussed first. These partnerships will extend to collaboration as fellow researchers as well as fellow practitioners. In the second section of this article, a few projected "challenge" themes for which these partnerships will be critical are provided.

TYPES OF PARTNERSHIPS AND OBJECTIVES

Four partnership areas are addressed below:

1. Theory building;
2. Data collection;
3. Generating interventions; and
4. Research/practitioner consortiums.

Theory Building

The internal focus of HR professionals and the external perspective of IO psychologists make for a potentially fruitful duo in terms of knowledge and insight. The unique perspective of each discipline must be proactively sought—each discipline from the other. As Katzell (1994) forewarns, this is an *insider-outsider* distinction, rather than the misleading *objective-subjective* distinction that is sometimes claimed. Often at issue, the scientific emphasis on control of the variables does not always serve the practitioner perspective, and therefore tradeoffs between research needs and practitioner nuances have to be weighed seriously, as will be discussed later. For generation of and refinement of theories, the day-to-day, insider perspective of the HR professional will serve to identify relevant variables and potential insights about new psychological dynamics as they emerge in tomorrow's workplace (for example, workers adapting to more diverse teams, virtual offices, and training technology). Human resources workers will need to be both generous and deliberate in sharing their insights so as to properly direct theoretical models and research endeavors.

For our part, IO psychologists will need to serve a constructive, devil's advocate role, rigorously testing the ideas generated by the HR perspective. In doing so, we should maintain an optimal balance between the two perspectives. To further complicate, but also to improve, our theory-building role, we will need to serve as brokers, assessing new ideas in light of theoretical models from our successful past research. Much of this literature is well-documented in the recent four volume series, *Handbook of Industrial Organizational Psychology* (see Dunnette & Hough, 1990–1992; Triandis, Dunnette, & Hough, 1994). The brokering role also extends to our need to integrate helpful models from other psychology subdivisions, particularly research in the area of cognition (DeNisi, Cafferty, & Meglino, 1984; Lord & Maher, 1991) and cross-cultural psychology (Erez, 1994; Kagitcibasi & Berry, 1989). This brokering role will be particularly challenging, as it will require an openness to new and unfamiliar work phenomena balanced with attentiveness to testing the fit of previously shaped and research-supported models with such novel work issues.

Finally, a supplemental note regarding the investigation of cross-cultural influences on workplace psychology is warranted. The exploration of new perspectives related to IO psychology with an international scope is barely beginning. However, some significant strides have been made (see Earley & Erez, 1997; Triandis, 1994) to infuse our discipline with important theoretical models and methodological foundations that introduce the factor of culture into the study of organizational behavior.

Data Collection

Both HR professionals and IO psychologists have codes of ethics to which they are committed. The sensitivity of collecting work-related information and the need to strike a balance between the often conflicting duality of scientific and practitioner objectives (Yorks & Whitsett, 1985) are heavy and time-consuming responsibilities. Although essential, these responsibilities may be excessively complicated and disputable in terms of fair expectations (Mirvis & Seashore, 1979). We cannot be presumptuous or lackadaisical about the sensitive nature of data gathering and interpretation. The need for careful attention is heightened when one is introducing cultural issues that involve discussion of data proposed to capture indices of a group's system of "shared meanings" (Shweder & Levine, 1984).

It would be tragic if understanding were to be inhibited due to collective myopia about the role of ethics in cross-cultural research. Therefore, representatives from both disciplines should engage in focused discussion and then document ethical obligations and expectations. This discourse would supplement, not replace, current ethical guidelines for each discipline and would provide each party with an enlightened view of the other's perspective and values.

In addition, a greater understanding of culture's role in how organizational interventions affect work processes and outcomes will require two types of extensions to the data-collection process. First, it will be necessary for both disciplines to create and contribute to larger data pools jointly. This could be done physically via a clearinghouse of data sets in which various cultures are represented and classified. The issue of how to classify and measure cultural values is and should continue to be paramount (Sego, Hui, & Law, 1997).

The statistical approach of meta-analyses (Glass, 1976) can promote greater understanding without requiring the raw data that harbors the aforementioned personal sensitivity issues. Meta-analysis is a powerful statistical strategy that has become somewhat of a specialization to IO psychologists, who use it both for reaching conclusions across multiple studies (McEvoy & Cascio, 1985) and as a practitioner tool for improving employee selection strategies (Hunter & Hunter, 1984). To reap the full benefits of meta-analyses in the future, organizations should find ways to communicate statistical relationships among their work variables (for example, between satisfaction and performance), many of which are quantified in employee surveys and other in-house data-collection projects. Improved HR information systems may make both the calculation and sharing of such information quite easy. Of course, confidentiality issues would have to be addressed.

Second, in order to more fully understand and "work with" cultural diversity, HR professionals and IO psychologists will need to become more open to, and creative with, alternative (non-quantitative) assessment methods, such as qualitative (Denzin & Lincoln, 1994) and eco-cultural (Berry, 1997) approaches. Although most of the data-collection efforts thus far have been couched in a research context, their application and relevance to practitioner issues, such as performance evaluation and feedback to individuals of varying cultures or cross-cultural team dynamics, should be quite obvious. Gibson (1997) provides a compelling overview of this overlap in terms of intercultural organizational communication.

Human resources functions can often be clearly conceptualized as a type of research or experimental task (Cascio, 1991; Senge, 1990). Therefore, it will be essential for both areas to reevaluate their methodological approaches continually. The processes of measurement and assessment will become more critical and more difficult in the near future. Change is, ironically, the one constant. However, the anticipated increase in the velocity of change will mean rethinking our assumptions when we develop, implement, and assess workplace interventions. Incorporation of chaos theory (Gleick, 1987; Katzell, 1994), nonlinear thinking and analyses, and more dynamic, temporal elements (such as the nature of work phenomena changing over an individual's tenure) will be required in order to understand and manage the future of work.

Generating Interventions

As suggested, vibrant and rigorous theory and research collaboration between HR and IO should lead to a fruitful harvest of applications. It is here where IO psychologists must continue to evolve as co-practitioners—assisting HR professionals in selecting, developing, implementing, and assessing the interventions that have the best fit. From our external consulting perspective, the IO psychologist should have knowledge and expertise to maximize the impact of interventions, as well as to anticipate and minimize the concerns and problems of implementing change mechanisms. Industrial/organizational psychologists should be looked to for insights: Which interventions work, how and why, under what conditions, and in what type of cultural (both organizational and national) contexts?

Research/Practitioner Consortiums

All three of the roles previously described are interrelated in a systematic, chronological sequence. Yet each step may require separate individuals or groups to assist in the task at hand, whether it be theory building, data collecting, or generating interventions. Consequently, it will become even more critical to have joint research efforts involving representatives from both HR and IO and to communicate the results in shared research mediums, such as journals and conferences. Collaborative efforts should be further facilitated by both areas' joint commitment and contribution to national and international forums, such as the human capital initiative currently coordinated by the American Psychological Society (National Behavioral Science Research Agenda Committee, 1992).

Similarly, the effects of globalization on organizational and individual outcomes will require an abundance of cross-cultural alliances. Graen, Hui, Wakabayashi, and Wang (1997) offer a stellar model and case study of cross-cultural research teams by proposing guidelines, roles, and developmental processes to manage and optimize the diverse talents and cultural worldviews inherent in such joint efforts. The researchers identify critical roles for different members and detail partnership-making strategies. In addition, Teagarden and colleagues (1995) share their insights from a successful multinational, multicultural, interdisciplinary research consortium by discussing strategies to overcome obstacles to comparative management research.

PROJECTED THEMES AND DIRECTIONS

Building Better Mouse Traps: Selection Challenges

Here the "mice" are potential employees with vital talents and aptitudes desired by competitive organizations. The "trap" represents the selection tool to best identify, attract, and retain that critical talent. This has been predicted to be the biggest challenge for HR professionals over the next few decades.

Globalization will continue to influence the selection of employees in two major ways. First, previously provincial applicant pools will span national borders and allow for the hiring of workers who may or may not physically relocate. Virtual offices are already a reality, with some tentative support for their effectiveness (Cascio, 1998). There is no reason to believe that telecommuting has to stop at a nation's borders.

Second, just as a progression to a "mesa" level of analysis—analyses from the individual employee to the socioeconomic environment (Cappelli & Sherer, 1991)—will change HR jobs, it will also complicate business practices for many others as well. Individuals will be dealing with customers, suppliers, co-workers, and even supervisors from different cultures. Employees will work interdependently with constituents who may be performing similar functions but with dramatically different styles.

In addition, unique organizational structures will mean interfacing with team structures and functional departments foreign to the individual. The information provided by target persons or groups will often be filled with nuances unique to their organizational or national cultures. This issue cannot be passed off with the naive notion that workers will eventually become familiar with their static job-related linkages. Environmental instability, demographic shifts, and increased international competition will pose a monumental challenge to long-term human resource planning (Jackson & Schuler, 1990). These new linkages within and between organizations and cultures call for valid and reliable selection strategies applicable to a broad spectrum of jobs:

- Systems thinking,

- Information handling,

- Managing ambiguity,

- Cultural sensitivity, and

- Trainability.

Industrial/organizational psychologists and HR professionals will need to work together to develop and validate measurement strategies that are sensitive to individual differences. It is clear that assessing these constructs will be difficult, but an emerging workforce with multiple aptitudes will contribute to a competitive edge for international businesses. Although it is beyond the scope of this article to review the preliminary work that has been done related to aptitudes, some preliminary work is underway. See the References section for some sources.

Systems Thinking

A definitive description of *systems thinking* is difficult, given the wide spectrum of relevant principles and proposed models available (Katzell, 1994). It would seem to require individuals to be able to conceptualize, organize, and interpret work phenomena (problems, interventions, action plans) from a perspective that encompasses multiple, interactive levels of analysis and with a sensitivity to the interdependence (often nonlinear) between levels and between components within each level. For example, an HR professional would have to recognize the impact of a motivational program instituted within one department on the rest of the organization. The recent inroads systems thinking has made into management cybernetics (Espejo, 1994), organizational learning (Checkland & Haynes, 1994; McKenna, 1992), organizational consultation (Fatzer, 1990), and other organizational dynamics (Kim & Senge, 1994; Senge, 1990) suggest the need to take a closer look at applicants' predisposition to engaging in this type of cognitive skill.

Information Handling

Information handling pertains to an individual's ability to organize, manage, and consolidate vast amounts of information from multiple sources, in varied modalities, and with chronically changing or revised content. Some of the models on task complexity (Campbell, 1988; Wood, 1986) and cognitive complexity (Hooijberg & Quinn, 1992; Streufert & Nogami, 1989) may provide helpful guides for constructing measures for this. Cognitive complexity as it is currently assessed has been shown to be a strong predictor of management performance in a turbulent business environment (McGill, Johnson, & Bantel, 1994).

Managing Ambiguity

The work scenario described earlier is fraught with uncertainty. Like conflict, *ambiguity* can be either devastating to a system or constructively managed. A great deal of work has been done with regard to measuring one's tolerance for ambiguity (Durrheim & Foster, 1997; McLain, 1993). However, "tolerance" will be insufficient for future workers. Work dynamics will require individuals to be able to manage the ambiguity with which they will be faced during cross-cultural communications (Gibson, 1997). Lin (1997) makes a compelling assertion that the power element within cross-cultural communication may exacerbate the ambiguity challenge. Thus, instruments are needed to assess the ability of future workers to manage ambiguity.

Cultural Sensitivity

The need for *cultural sensitivity* among workers is blatantly obvious. International organizations will need to be well-staffed with what Graen and colleagues (1997) refer to as "transculturals" or "cultural sensitizers." These are individuals who have an ability to learn and conform to the behavioral norms of another country. Reeves-Ellington (1995) documents a remarkable success story of using an ethnic group model for developing a global organization partially by paying attention to cultural sensitivity among its workers.

Trainability

Trainability is similar to the general aptitude that most cognitive ability tests capture. However, factors such as trainee motivation, commitment to the philosophy of the learning organization, self-directed learning potential, and adaptability to multiple modes of training must be better understood (Hayes & Allinson, 1997). Our work will need to build on the conceptual work that Goldstein (1991) outlines as part of the preconditions to training. The increased complexity and reliance on training systems (discussed in the next section) is further evidence of the need to ensure that incoming workers are train-able.

The discussion so far begs the questions: How do we measure such constructs? and Which measurement strategies will provide the best assessment for the criteria? Different selection instruments will have to be developed creatively for assessing these aptitudes (Mumford & Stokes, 1992). For instance, biographical information or patterns, structured and situational interview formats, computer simulations, or creative work samples may provide rich sources of information about employee aptitudes. In addition, cultural biases or preferences should be considered during the development of measurement tools. The key to success will be collaborative dialogue between HR professionals and IO psychologists. There is no definitive answer to the "How?" question yet. But business success will rely on practitioners' ability to make better selection decisions among diverse global applicant pools and hire workers who will enter their jobs with a greater readiness for the imminent rapid pace of change.

One last note on selection challenges: There is a projected need for future HR efforts to adjust the workplace to the worker (Minehan, 1998) at the time of hire. The presence of rare talent will necessitate HR to be ready to react to applicant requests for work redesign and other types of modifications. This will require a more transactional approach to selection than has been achieved previously. Industrial/organizational psychology can assist in shifting the focus of work redesign strategies to being part of the hiring process rather than after the fact.

It may be argued that some of the aptitudes discussed above need not be sought during the selection process, as workers could be trained later. Perhaps—but I would argue against leaving these issues exclusively to training, an already overburdened function. The abstract nature of these aptitudes may be somewhat malleable, but individual differences have more likely been shaped by socialization, particularly education—and therefore applicants will bring a fairly stable level of each of these aptitudes with them. Training, no doubt, will be a critical HR-IO research-practice issue; and so we turn now to it.

Leading the Horses to Water and Getting Them to Drink: Training Challenges

Dramatic effects are being felt in education from technology manifested through virtual classrooms and distance learning. The use of technology for training purposes in the world of business will be even more widespread and dramatic in the future (Minehan, 1998). It has been predicted that technology will provide two valuable benefits to the area of training: (1) It will make training more available to a broader population of workers and more frequently accessible to any one individual worker and (2) it will allow for greater "learning flexibility," as it will provide formats (lecture, demonstration, modeling, simulation) and modalities (visual, auditory, interactive) that will adjust to the needs, abilities, and cognitive styles of the individual trainee (Hayes & Allinson, 1997). Used correctly, the technology will be like an injection of adrenaline to bolster the trainee's motivation to learn. Training systems will have to be designed to evoke such a response from workers. This will require interdisciplinary efforts from educational specialists, cognitive psychologists, human factors, computer scientists, and, yes, IO psychologists and HR professionals.

The multiple ways technology will facilitate a growth in training programs is mind-boggling. The image of the current attempt to fully harness the applications in this area is a stampede of horses pushing onward, often not fully in control. A concerted, interdisciplinary approach, in which HR and IO are only two of many key players, will yield innovations that will achieve several outcomes:

- Bolster the aptitudes discussed above;

- Promote personal growth and better balance to the work/family dilemmas discussed below; and

- Be a key to bringing many of the ideal principles of Senge's (1990) learning organization to fruition.

Quinones and Ehrenstein (1997) provide an extended discussion of this theme and other future challenges to the training function.

Accentuate the Positives, Eliminate the Negatives, Latch on to the Affirmative: The Challenge of the Psychological Contract

According to Minehan (1998, p. 81), "Employers will need to put more emphasis on adjusting the workplace to the needs of employees," ensuring their more positive approach to work, minimizing the negative aspects of work demands, and thus affirming the whole individual. This trend is essential for practical reasons—to attract and retain a desirable, healthy workforce—and is consistent with other common ideals—contributing to the social good and promotion of fuller personal growth. This will be a mammoth challenge to employers because it will rely on the suitability of the perceived psychological contract between employee and employer. This psychological contract consists of the beliefs about the reciprocal obligations between that employee and his or her employer (Morrison & Robinson, 1997).

Because it is rooted in the psychology of the individual employee (based on his or her perceptions, emotions, and cognitive schemas), it can often lead to extremely negative reactions by that individual when violated. It is difficult for an organization to monitor and manage the psychological contract due to its idiosyncratic nature. Also, substantive evolutions in personnel patterns as a function of shifts in demographics throughout the world have deeply hurt many citizens by demanding of them grueling transitions, causing them to reassess their conception of the employment relationship (Rousseau, 1997).

Thus, employers must pay careful attention to the psychological contract for several reasons, such as the following. *Congruence* between employer and employee expectations relative to the psychological contract has been shown to be positively associated with many desirable work outcomes, including organizational commitment and job satisfaction (Scandura & Lankau, 1997), retention of expatriate managers (Guzzo, Noonan, & Elron, 1994), improved learning climates (Sims, 1992), and stress reduction in the employee socialization process (Nelson, Quick, & Joplin, 1991). *Incongruence* has been speculated to be associated with employee feelings of anger, betrayal (Morrison & Robinson, 1997), and possibly subsequent violence (Johnson & Indvik, 1994).

These findings are just the tip of the iceberg for what will be empirically revealed about the effects of managing or mismanaging the psychological contract on the productivity and well-being of tomorrow's workforce. Seeing failure as a function of an organization's inability to adapt to changing economic circumstances, Levinson (1994) suggests the problems are fundamentally rooted in the psychological contract. Levinson states: "The explanations are fundamentally psychological, significantly having to do with individual and organizational narcissism, unconscious recapitulation of family dynamics in the organization, exacerbating dependency, psychologically illogical organization structure and compensation schemes, inadequate management of change, and inability to recognize and manage cognitive complexity" (p. 428).

Human resources professionals and IO psychologists will be in the trenches battling many of the organizational forces and will need to co-develop mechanisms to circumvent some of these counterproductive organizational forces. At the same time, they will need to somehow promote simultaneous individual *and* organizational transformation. Understanding the role of the psychological contract and developing mechanisms to facilitate congruence will be crucial steps in these endeavors.

To close, it is important to note that these are only a few of many potential areas espoused from just one IO psychology perspective. Similar themes can be developed in performance appraisal, leadership development, motivation, and a host of other areas, such as in the research agenda outlined by Cascio (1995). This paper simply serves as a beckoning for HR-IO partnerships to continue to blossom and grow, so as to face the turbulent winds of change confronting the well-being of business.

References and Resources

American Psychological Association. (1981). Specialty guidelines for the delivery of services by industrial/ organizational psychologists. *American Psychologist, 36*(6), 664–669.

Berry, J.W. (1997). An ecocultural approach to the study of cross-cultural industrial/ organizational psychology. In P.C. Early & M. Erez (Eds.), *New perspectives on international industrial/organizational psychology* (pp. 130–147). San Francisco, CA: The New Lexington Press.

Campbell, D.J. (1988, January). Task complexity: A review and analysis. *Academy of Management Review, 13*(1), 40–52.

Cappelli, P., & Sherer, P.D. (1991). The missing role of context in OB: The need for a meso-level approach. In L.L Cummings & B.M. Staw (Eds.), *Research in organizational behavior* (Vol. 13, pp. 55–110). Greenwich, CT: JAI Press.

Cascio, W.F. (1991). *Applied psychology in personnel management* (4th ed.). Upper Saddle River, NJ: Prentice Hall.

Cascio, W.F. (1995, November). Whither industrial and organizational psychology in a changing world of work? *American Psychologist, 50*(11), 928–939.

Cascio, W.F. (1998). The virtual workplace: A reality now. *The Industrial-Organizational Psychologist, 35*(4), 32–36.

Checkland, P.B., & Haynes, M.G. (1994). Varieties of systems thinking: The case of soft systems methodology. [Special Issue: Systems thinkers, systems thinking]. *System Dynamics Review, 10*(2–3), 189–197.

DeNisi, A.S., Cafferty, T.P., & Meglino, B.M. (1984, June). A cognitive view of the performance appraisal process: A model and research proposition. *Organizational Behavior and Human Performance, 33*(3), 360–396.

Denzin, N.K., & Lincoln, Y.S. (Eds.). (1994). *Handbook of qualitative research.* Thousand Oaks, CA: Sage.

Dunnette, M.D., & Hough, L.M. (Eds.). (1990–1992). *Handbook of industrial and organizational psychology* (Vols. 1-3). (2nd ed.). Palo Alto, CA: Consulting Psychologists Press.

Durrheim, K., & Foster, D. (1997). Tolerance of ambiguity as a content specific construct. *Personality and Individual Differences, 22*(5), 741–750.

Earley, P.C., & Erez, M. (Eds.). (1997). *New perspectives on international industrial/ organizational psychology.* San Francisco, CA: The New Lexington Press.

Erez, M. (1994). Toward a model of cross-cultural industrial and organizational psychology. In H.C. Triandis, M.D. Dunnette, & L.M. Hough (Eds.), *Handbook of industrial/organizational psychology* (Vol. 4, pp. 559–608). Palo Alto, CA: Consulting Psychologists Press.

Espejo, R. (1994). What is systemic thinking? [Special Issue: Systems thinkers, systems thinking]. *System Dynamics Review, 10*(2–3), 199–212.

Fatzer, G. (1990). Systemdenken als neues paradigma der arbiet mit organizationen (Systems thinking as a new paradigm for organizational consultation). *Gruppendynamik, 21*(1), 45–59.

Gibson, C.B. (1997). Do you hear what I hear? A framework for reconciling intercultural communication difficulties arising from cognitive styles and cultural values. In P.C. Early & M. Erez (Eds.), *New perspectives on international industrial/organizational psychology* (pp. 335–362). San Francisco, CA: The New Lexington Press.

Glass, C.V. (1976, November). Primary, secondary, and meta-analysis of research. *Educational Research*, pp. 3–8.

Gleick, J. (1987). *Explorations in managerial talent.* Pacific Palisades, CA: Goodyear.

Goldstein, I.L. (1991). Training in work organizations. In M.D. Dunnette & L.M. Hough (Eds.), *Handbook of industrial and organizational psychology* (2nd ed.) (Vol. 2, pp. 507–619). Palo Alto, CA: Consulting Psychologists Press.

Graen, G.B., Hui, C., Wakabayashi, M., & Wang, Z.M. (1997). Cross-cultural research alliances in organizational research: Cross-cultural partnership-making in action. In P.C. Early & M. Erez (Eds.), *New perspectives on international industrial/organizational psychology* (pp. 160–190). San Francisco, CA: The New Lexington Press.

Guterman, M.S. (1994). *Common sense for uncommon times: The power of balance in work, family, and personal life.* Palo Alto, CA: Consulting Psychologists Press.

Guzzo, R.A., Noonan, K.A., & Elron, E. (1994). Expatriate managers and the psychological contract. *Journal of Applied Psychology, 79*(4), 617–626.

Hayes, J., & Allinson, C.W. (1997). Learning styles and training and development in work settings: Lessons from educational research. *Educational Psychology, 17*(1–2), 185–193.

Hooijberg, R., & Quinn, R.E. (1992). Behavioral complexity and the development of effective managers. In R.L. Phillips & J.G. Hunt (Eds.), *Strategic leadership: A multiorganizational-level perspective* (pp. 161–175). Westport, CT: Quorum Books.

Howard, A. (1995). *The changing nature of work.* San Francisco, CA: Jossey-Bass.

Hunter, J.E., & Hunter, R.F. (1984, September). Validity and utility of alternative predictors of job performance. *Psychological Bulletin, 96*(2), 72–98.

Jackson, S.E., & Schuler, R.S. (1990). Human resource planning: Challenges for industrial/organizational psychologists. *American Psychologist, 45*(2), 223–239.

Johnson, P.R., & Indvik, J. (1994). Workplace violence: An issue of the nineties. *Public Personnel Management, 23*(4), 515–523.

Kagitcibasi, C., & Berry, J.W. (1989). Cross cultural psychology: Current research and trends. *Annual Review of Psychology, 40,* 493–531.

Katzell, R.A. (1994). Contemporary meta-trends in industrial and organizational psychology. In H.C. Triandis, M.D. Dunnette, & L.M. Hough (Eds.), *Handbook of industrial/organizational psychology* (Vol. 4, pp. 1–94). Palo Alto, CA: Consulting Psychologists Press.

Kim, D.H., & Senge, P.M. (1994). Putting systems thinking into practice. [Special Issue: Systems thinkers, systems thinking]. *System Dynamic Review, 10*(2–3), 277–290.

Levinson, H. (1994). Why the behemoths fell: Psychological roots of corporate failure. *American Psychologist, 49*(5), 428–436.

Lin, Z. (1997). Ambiguity with a purpose: The shadow of power in communication. In P.C. Early & M. Erez (Eds.), *New perspectives on international industrial/organizational psychology* (pp. 363–376). San Francisco, CA: The New Lexington Press.

Lord, R.G., & Maher, K.J. (1991). Cognitive theory in industrial and organizational psychology. In M.D. Dunnette & L.M. Hough (Eds.), *Handbook of industrial and organizational psychology* (2nd ed.) (Vol. 2, pp. 1–62). Palo Alto, CA: Consulting Psychologists Press.

May, K.E. (1998). Work in the 21st century: The changing role of human resources. *The Industrial-Organizational Psychologist, 35*(3), 28–31.

McEvoy, G.M., & Cascio, W.F. (1985, February). Strategies for reducing employee turnover: A meta-analysis. *Journal of Applied Psychology, 70*(1), 342–353.

McGill, A.R., Johnson, M.D., & Bantel, K.A. (1994). Cognitive complexity and conformity: Effects on performance in a turbulent environment. *Psychological Reports, 73*(3, Pt. 2), 1451–1472.

McKenna, S.D. (1992). A culture instrument: Driving organizational learning. *Leadership and Organization Development Journal, 13*(6), 24–29.

McLain, D.L. (1993). The MSTAT-I: A new measure of an individual's tolerance for ambiguity. *Educational and Psychological Measurement, 53*(1), 183–189.

Minehan, M. (1998). Futurist task force. *HR Magazine, 43*(3), 77–84, 188–190.

Mirvis, P.H., & Seashore, S.E. (1979, September). Being ethical in organizational research. *American Psychologist, 34*(9), 766–780.

Morrison, E.W., & Robinson, S.L. (1997). When employees feel betrayed: A model of how psychological contract violation develops. *Academy of Management Review, 22*(1), 226–256.

Mumford, M.D., & Stokes, G.S. (1992). Developmental determinants of individual action: Theory and practice in applying background measures. In M.D. Dunnette & L.M. Hough (Eds.), *Handbook of industrial and organizational psychology* (2nd ed.) (Vol. 3, pp. 61–138). Palo Alto, CA: Consulting Psychologists Press.

National Behavioral Science Research Agenda Committee. (1992, February). Human capital initiative [Special issue]. *APS Observer.*

Nelson, D.L., Quick, J.C., & Joplin, J.R. (1991). Psychological contracting and newcomer socialization: An attachment theory foundation. [Special Issue: Handbook on job stress]. *Journal of Social Behavior and Personality, 6*(7), 55–72.

Quinones, M.A., & Ehrenstein, A. (Eds.). (1997). *Training for a rapidly changing workplace: Applications of psychological research.* Washington, DC: American Psychological Association.

Reeves-Ellington, R. (1995). Organizing for global effectiveness: Ethnicity and organizations. *Human Organization, 54*(3), 249–262.

Rousseau, D.M. (1997). Organizational behavior in the new organizational era. *Annual Review of Psychology, 48*(1), 515–546.

Scandura, T.A., & Lankau, M.J. (1997). Relationships of gender, family responsibility and flexible work hours to organizational commitment and job satisfaction. *Journal of Organizational Behavior, 18*(4), 377–391.

Sego, D.J., Hui, C., & Law, K.S. (1997). Operationalizing cultural values as the mean of individual values: Problems and suggestions for research. In P.C. Early & M. Erez (Eds.), *New perspectives on international industrial/organizational psychology* (pp. 148–159). San Francisco, CA: The New Lexington Press.

Senge, P.M. (1990). *The fifth discipline: The art and practice of the learning organization.* New York: Currency Doubleday.

Shweder, R.A., & Levine, R.A. (1984). *Culture theory: Essays on mind, self, and emotion.* New York: Cambridge University Press.

Sims, R.R. (1992). Developing the learning climate in public sector training programs. *Public Personnel Management, 21*(3), 335–346.

Streufert, S., & Nogami, G.Y. (1989). Cognitive style and complexity: Implications for I/O psychology. In C.L. Cooper & I.T. Robertson (Eds.), *International review of industrial and organizational psychology* (pp. 93–143). Chichester, England: John Wiley & Sons.

Teagarden, M.B., Von Glinow, M.A., Bowen, D.E., Frayne, C.A., et al. (1995). Toward a theory of comparative management research: An idiographic case study of the best international human resources management project. *Academy of Management Journal, 38*(5), 1261–1287.

Triandis, H.C. (1994). Cross-cultural industrial and organizational psychology. In H.C. Triandis, M.D. Dunnette, & L.M. Hough (Eds.), *Handbook of industrial/organizational psychology* (Vol. 4, pp. 103–172). Palo Alto, CA: Consulting Psychologists Press.

Triandis, H.C., Dunnette, M.D., & Hough, L.M. (Eds.). (1994). *Handbook of industrial/organizational psychology.* Palo Alto, CA: Consulting Psychologists Press.

Wood, R.E. (1986, February). Task complexity: Definition of the construct. *Organizational Behavior and Human Decision Processes, 37*(1), 60–82.

Yorks, L., & Whitsett, D.A. (1985, January). Hawthorne, Topeka, and the issue of science versus advocacy in organizational behavior. *Academy of Management Review, 10*(1), 21–30.

Robert T. Brill, Ph.D., *is an associate professor of psychology at Moravian College, Bethlehem, Pennsylvania, where he is director of the Human Resources Certificate Program and the industrial/organizational psychology track of the psychology bachelor's degree. He has taught courses in industrial, organizational, and social psychology, as well as in statistics and research methodology. He has undertaken many consulting and research projects in the areas of selection, training, communication, performance appraisal, and employee well-being.*

THE ABC'S OF STRATEGIC MANAGEMENT^{SM}: THE SYSTEMS THINKING APPROACH^{SM} TO CREATING A CUSTOMER-FOCUSED, HIGH-PERFORMANCE ORGANIZATION

Stephen G. Haines

Abstract: This article discusses applying systems thinking as a new organizational orientation. In particular, the application of systems thinking to strategic planning results in the reinvention of strategic planning as a more holistic system of strategic management.

Based on systems thinking, the natural way the world works, the A-B-C-D-E "core technology" explained in this article has been proven by the author's global alliance in over sixteen countries to work for organizations of all types.

Three main premises and three goals of strategic management are presented in this article that the author claims separate it from all other strategic planning processes of the past.

Thinking Backward to the Future

In the Industrial Age, public and private enterprises built their future by incremental expansion of technology, assumptions, and day-to-day operations. In today's global Information Age, merely building on the present is no longer a viable strategy. Worldwide markets and instant global communications are now multiplying all our opportunities.

Today, organizations must keep pace with changes in their environment and reduce current expenses, waste, and bureaucratic operations. They must completely reinvent their future vision and then begin thinking backward to this future with the strategies needed to remain successful. They must commit passionately to the disciplined management of the changes that occur along the way toward becoming a customer-focused, high-performance, learning organization.

The ABC's of Strategic Management^{SM}

My work has led me to look for simple, yet systematic, ways to focus on strategic management (both for planning and for change). As a result, I've clarified and simplified these ideas into a strategic management system with three goals:

Goal 1.   Develop a strategic plan and document it.

Goal 2.   Ensure successful implementation.

Goal 3.   Build and sustain high performance.

To achieve these goals, it is important to gain an understanding of the three premises that were the basis for strategic management in the past:

Premise 1. Planning and Change Are a Primary Part of Management and Leadership. Strategic management must culminate in a significant change in the way leaders conduct their business day to day. This is a key difference between our model and others, which tend to suffer the fatal "SPOTS" syndrome (strategic plans on top shelves—gathering dust). Having strategic planning and change led by top management is a critical requirement to achieve the three goals above. Strategic plans are the blueprints; executives must fill in implementation details.

Premise 2. People Support What They Help Create.   A core planning team of eight to fifteen people from your collective leadership should head the strategic management process, do the hard work, and make the tough decisions. A crucial planning and change team task is to involve the rest of management and key stakeholders in a meaningful way, gathering their input on all draft documents and increasing their ownership of the plan.

Visionary and participative leadership practices that produce dynamic leaders, as opposed to the feared bosses of the past, is a necessity as we enter the 21st Century. Leaders must be trainers, coaches, and facilitators to carry out this process.

Premise 3. Customer-Focused Systems Thinking Is Required.   Systems thinking provides some very clear elements and answers for how to become a successful organization over the long term. While there is no single answer or Holy Grail to be found, every organization, whether public or private, needs to become an outcome-oriented system, focused on the customer.

The Systems Thinking Approach described here provides a framework for a successful strategic management model. A *system* is defined as a set of components that work together toward the overall objective of the whole. Our systems model is comprised of five distinct components or phases (A-B-C-D-E) (see Figure 1), the ABCs of systems thinking. Any system can be described by the following phases: a series of inputs (Phase C) to a throughput or actions (Phase D) to achieve your outputs (Phase A) along with a feedback loop (Phase B) in the environment (Phase E) to measure success.

The ABC systems phases start with A (as we want to be proactive in creating our ideal future) instead of C, the traditional left-to-right flow. Once you create a future, you work backward to today to make it happen.

This strategic management model has been reinvented based on research in general systems theory, the author's own experiences as an executive and consultant, and continual practical application and refinement from clients who have used it. Additionally, a literature search and comparative analysis of twenty-seven other popular strategic management models was done. The element missing from all other models was discovered to be the systems focus on outcomes and on the customer.

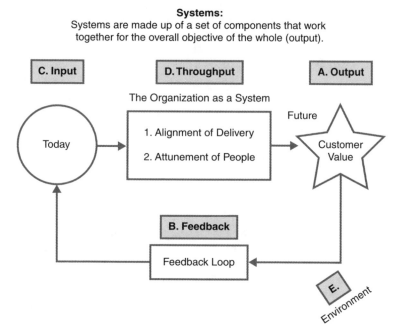

From Complexity to Simplicity

Systems:
Systems are made up of a set of components that work
together for the overall objective of the whole (output).

Figure 1. The Five-Phase Systems Model

Following is a more detailed explanation of the phases in the model.

Phase E. Environmental Scan

Begin with the *plan-to-plan* step prior to Phase A. We will not normally contract with a client to undertake overall strategic management before this innovative initial step is taken. It is composed of five elements:

1. An environmental scan (Phase E);

2. An organizational assessment;

3. Visionary leadership practices, skills, and team-building training for the CEO, top executives, and middle management;

4. Establishing and training an internal support cadre; and

5. A one-day executive briefing and organizing session.

This skill building for the leadership of the organization is crucial, as leadership is the *only* thing that really differentiates firms from each other *over the long term*.

The last item of the planning step—the one-day executive briefing session—also called an "educating, organizing, and tailoring" day—ensures that everyone has the same understanding of the model and the terminology. The organizational assessment leads to a joint tailoring of a strategic planning process that makes sense to the executives involved. Even if strategic planning is not pursued, this plan-to-plan step is valuable in its own right as a unique diagnostic and learning event.

Once the plan-to-plan phase is completed, then the ABCs of strategic planning and change begin in earnest.

Phase A. Output (Creating Your Ideal Future)

This step begins with a scanning of the desired future environment. However, the main purpose is to formulate dreams that are worth believing in and fighting for. At this stage, the cry of "It can't be done!" is irrelevant; the issue of how to turn the vision into reality will be pursued after the vision is created. The four challenges met during this phase are as follows:

- *Challenge 1.* Conduct a visioning process and develop a shared vision statement of the organization's dreams, hopes, and desired future.

- *Challenge 2.* Develop a mission statement describing why the organization exists, what business it is in, and who it serves.

- *Challenge 3.* Articulate core values that guide day-to-day behavior and, collectively, create a desired culture.

- *Challenge 4.* Develop a rallying cry and position statement—a crisp and concise statement of the entire strategic plan and the organization's competitive edge.

Phase B. Feedback (Measurements of Success)

During this phase two elements are developed: (1) the key factors for achieving an organization's vision, mission, and core values on a year-by-year basis and (2) the measures by which success will be determined. The maximum preferred number of key success factors is ten, forcing a focus on what's really "key" to success. Key success factors should always measure what's really important (not just what's easy to measure) including, at a minimum, customer satisfaction, employee satisfaction, and financial viability.

Phase C. Input (Converting Strategy to Operations)

The first part of this phase is the *current state assessment,* where internal and external analyses of strengths, weaknesses, opportunities, and threats (SWOTs) are conducted.

In traditional forms of strategic management, this step is the first step, leading to long-range planning that projects the current state into the future. However, the key is to assess today in light of your desired ideal future, not just to assess today in light of today.

The second step in this phase is *strategy development,* where the core strategies are created to bridge the gap between the ideal future vision and the current state assessment, resulting in three to seven core strategies to be implemented organization-wide (less is more).

The late 1990s saw a proliferation of new strategies as businesses tried to cope with these revolutionary times. Beware of those that focus only on cutting costs, such as reorganizations, layoffs, business reengineering, budget cutbacks, and so forth. "Cutting" is definitely necessary, yet not sufficient for success. "Building for the future" strategies, focused on quality products, services, and the Internet, and strategies that satisfy the customer are where the strategic answers are found. Thus, *both cutting and building strategies* are absolutely necessary.

Each core strategy you choose requires the development of action steps that will lead to success. Further, you must identify the top three to five priorities for each strategy over the next twelve months. These priorities become the organizing framework used by everyone in the company to set departmental plans and individual goals.

Developing annual plans and strategic budgeting is where "the rubber meets the road." It is where the company prioritizes action steps and budgets the resources to implement the core strategies. Individual unit plans are not adequate. A large group meeting of the top thirty to fifty leaders is needed to critique and refine drafts of plans based on their fit with top priorities of the organization as a whole.

It is also time to change the way budgeting is traditionally done. The budget must follow (not lead) annual planning. "Strategic budgeting" enables organizations to allocate resources based on the strategic plan in order to undertake the action steps set for the upcoming fiscal year. The tension created between current allocations and future priorities is normal and desired, as leaders are now forced to make the tough choices required for success.

Prior to Phase D (Another Pre-Planning Step)

The *plan-to-implement* step, the bridge from Goal 1 to Goal 2, is accomplished during a one-day session. Key are the following crucial concepts:

1. Creation of a strategic change leadership steering committee.
2. Development of a yearly comprehensive implementation map.
3. Assignment of cross-functional strategy sponsorship teams.
4. Selection of an internal change management support cadre.
5. Finalization of and rollout of the strategic plan.
6. Assignment of someone responsible for tracking key success factors.
7. Allocation of resources to support the change process/priorities.
8. Presentation of senior executives' personal leadership plans.
9. Modification of performance appraisal and rewards processes for employees to align with the new plan.
10. Development of a game plan to ensure a critical mass for change.
11. Creation of the "people edge."
12. Alignment of the delivery processes.

Phase D. Throughput (Implementation)

This phase has two parts. First is *strategy implementation and change*, the beginning of accomplishing Goal 2: ensure successful implementation. This phase transforms the strategic plan into thousands of individual plans and ties a rewards system to it. The organization's performance appraisal system is used to evaluate everyone on current behaviors versus the core organizational values and on their contribution to results.

Implicit in this part of the process is the understanding that change must be managed before it manages us (in ways we may not like). Quarterly or bi-monthly meetings of a strategic change leadership steering committee are absolutely essential. No organization we have worked with has successfully implemented its strategic plan without such a steering committee.

In addition, the CEO must conduct weekly meetings with his or her staff to review the status of the top priorities for each core strategy previously agreed to (with internal support cadre help).

Implementation needs to focus on the vital few leverage points for strategic change. These leverage points are (1) leadership and management practices attuned with peoples' hearts and minds; (2) customer-focused, business process reengineering to eliminate waste, that is, alignment of the delivery system; and (3) becoming more customer-focused through improved high-quality products and services.

Last is a need for an *annual strategic review* (and update), similar to an independent financial audit, to help the organization keep pace with and be flexible in response to a changing environment. This is the key to Goal 3: building and sustaining high performance over the long term. It includes the following points:

1. Reacting to changes in the environment (Phase E).
2. Formally auditing and reviewing the strategic plan.
3. Conducting an organizational assessment.
4. Updating annual action priorities.
5. Implementing the strategic management system itself as the new way to run the business day to day.

How to Start

Listed below are five options for getting started with the strategic management process in your own organization.

- *Option A.* A one-day executive briefing and plan-to-plan event. (This is the educating, organizing, and tailoring day mentioned earlier.)
- *Option B.* A one-day plan-to-implement day. On this day, you would complete the twelve tasks listed earlier and later finish other aspects of the full strategic management process.
- *Option C.* Conduct training on strategic planning or strategic change.
- *Option D.* Because the system is continuous, you may actually enter it and begin the process at any point during the year. Thus, you could begin developing a system of managing strategically at whatever point you desire. This might mean starting with the strategic review and assessment, beginning a strategic change project you have in mind (such as total quality), developing your measures, doing a SWOT analysis, or whatever you desire.
- *Option E.* Conduct only the step you need now. The key is just to start!

Resources

Ackoff, R. (1974). *Redesigning the future: A systems approach to societal problems*. New York: John Wiley & Sons.

Ackoff, R. (1991). *Ackoff's fables: Irreverent reflections on business and bureaucracy*. New York: John Wiley & Sons.

Davidson, M. (1983). *Uncommon sense: The life and times of Ludwig Von Bertalanffy*. Los Angeles, CA: J.P. Tarcher.

Forrester, J.W. (1971). *Principles of systems*. Norwalk, CT: Productivity Press.

Miller, E.J., & Rice, A.K. (1967). *Systems of organization*. London: Tavistock.

Miller, J.G. (1995). *Living systems*. Boulder, CO: University Press of Colorado.

Mintzberg, H. (1994). *The rise and fall of strategic planning*. New York: The Free Press.

Mintzberg, H., Ahlstrand, B., & Lampel, J. (1998). *Strategy safari: A guided tour through the wilds of strategic management*. New York: The Free Press.

Mintzberg, H., & Quinn, J.B. (1992). *The strategy process concepts and contexts*. Upper Saddle River, NJ: Prentice Hall.

Vickers, G. (Ed.). (1972). A classification of systems. *Yearbook of the society for general systems research/academy of management research*. Washington, DC: Society for General Systems Research/Academy of Management.

Von Bertalanffy, L. (1968). *General systems theory*. New York: Brazille.

Stephen G. Haines *is a CEO, entrepreneur, and strategist. He has over twenty-five years of experience working closely with over two hundred CEOs. He is a U.S. Naval Academy graduate, has a master's degree in OD from George Washington University, and has completed doctoral work in educational psychology at Temple University in Philadelphia. Mr. Haines is president and founder of both the Centre for Strategic Management (a global alliance of master consultants and trainers) and its sister company, Systems Thinking Press. He was previously president and part-owner of the University Associates Consulting and Training Group.*

HOW TO RETAIN
HIGH-PERFORMANCE EMPLOYEES

Beverly Kaye and Sharon Jordan-Evans

Abstract: Keeping high-performing employees has become a top priority for today's organizations. A two-year study by the authors reveals that managers, supervisors, and team leaders play the greatest role in employee satisfaction or dissatisfaction. Today's employees want challenging and meaningful work, opportunities to learn and grow, the sense of being part of a group, and a good boss. This article describes the things that managers and supervisors can do to create these conditions and be "good bosses" in order to contribute to employee satisfaction and retention.

The Tide Has Turned

The tide has turned. No longer can employers tell employees, "Like it or leave it." Unemployment is at a thirty-year low, and a shortage of labor is expected to last over the next decade. In today's marketplace, attracting and retaining good employees is a top priority in both large and small organizations. In fact, it is the biggest concern of nearly one-half of today's CEOs, according to a study by the executive recruiting firm Transearch. With the cost of replacing workers at 70 percent to 200 percent of their annual salaries—not including the effects on the organization of lost knowledge, declining morale and productivity, and customer dissatisfaction—it is no surprise that four out of five respondents rated employee retention as a serious or very serious issue in a survey conducted by the American Management Association (1997).

Of course, today's workers expect fair pay and competitive benefits. They also are interested in job location and job security. But these are not the factors that keep them at the job once they are recruited.

Managers and human resource professionals who are familiar with the work of Abraham Maslow (1943, 1970) and Frederick Herzberg and his associates (1966) will not be surprised to hear that once employees have attained a level of competence that allows them to provide for their physical needs, salary and benefits rarely are the prime factors in job satisfaction and retention. A study by the Hay Group (1998) reports that out of fifty retention factors, pay is the least important to one-half million employees from over three hundred companies. With today's low unemployment figures and the constant recruitment efforts of competitors, this means that keeping one's best employees has become a serious organizational concern.

Responsibility Lies with the "Boss"

The authors conducted a two-year survey of over three thousand individuals in various job roles and industries. It revealed that managers, supervisors, team leaders, and project leaders—those individuals who lead and interact directly with employees—have the greatest impact on employees' satisfaction or dissatisfaction with their jobs. In short, "problems with the boss" is the primary reason that employees seek work elsewhere. The factors that drive employee satisfaction and commitment are largely within the control of the manager, supervisor, or team leader.

Four Primary Factors

The authors' study revealed the primary factors that contribute to retention as well as the managerial behaviors that create loyalty on the part of high-performing employees. These positive factors and behaviors can be placed in four categories: challenging and meaningful work, opportunities to learn and grow, the sense of being part of a group or team, and having a good boss. Of course, there is some overlap between these categories, especially between the first three and having a good boss, as the boss usually has some control over the other three factors.

Challenging and Meaningful Work

Exciting and challenging work and meaningful work that makes a difference or a contribution to society were cited as some of the most important factors in job satisfaction. These may be related to another important factor, the need to feel connected to a group or team, in that they reveal a desire to feel connected to one's work and to the larger society through one's work. If one is going to spend a great deal of one's life doing something, it at least should have some interest and some meaning or purpose.

The need for connection extends both from the work and to the work. One way in which connection and commitment to the work is developed is by having some say in how the work is done. This includes being able to influence or suggest improvements in work assignments, processes, schedules, and measurements.

Having autonomy and a sense of control over one's work are other very important factors reported by the study group. People whose bosses micromanage and/or fail to delegate generally feel frustrated. Taking responsibility for one's own work is a source of satisfaction for most workers. Even more satisfying is perceiving and meeting challenges on the job. This keeps the work exciting and instills a sense of pride in one's accomplishments.

Many employees, especially those in high-tech jobs, report that keeping up with knowledge and technology in the field is very important to them. This leads us to the second factor.

Opportunities to Learn and Grow

Career growth, learning, and development are three of the top reasons that people stay in their current jobs. A "good" boss provides opportunities for learning, challenges, and growth on the job that match the employee's abilities and aspirations. He or she encourages employees to improve the work itself as well as their skills and to keep up with the latest developments in their field.

Providing formal training and development opportunities is only one means of helping employees to learn and grow. Coaching, mentoring, and providing informal learning opportunities on the job can be done regularly. Employees also should be encouraged to "network," to join trade and professional associations, and to read publications related to their lines of work.

The Sense of Being Part of a Group or Team

Working with great people, being part of a team, and having fun on the job are some other important factors in job satisfaction. These factors relate to the human need to feel connected. The proliferation and success of formal work teams can be attributed, in part, to this need. The work team, if managed well, also can help to meet this need.

Even a department, section, or division can feel like a "team" if the manager and employees treat one another with courtesy and respect, listen to one another's ideas, recognize and celebrate one another's accomplishments, and work toward common goals. Of course, every team or work group can benefit from training in areas such as communication, group development, consensus decision making, planning, and conflict resolution. It is the manager's responsibility to provide the work group members or team members with the tools and resources to work well together. It is the group's responsibility to utilize them well. For example, being comfortable enough with one's co-workers to solicit peer feedback goes a long way toward helping employees to feel trust, connection, and satisfaction in their work groups.

A Good Boss

Most managers and supervisors realize that the following behaviors will not earn the loyalty or respect of their employees: rudeness, impatience, arrogance, intimidation, yelling, being condescending or demeaning, belittling or embarrassing people, swearing, telling lies, sexual harassment, using inappropriate humor, and demonstrating sexism or racism.

They may or may not realize that the following behaviors or practices can be equally destructive to good boss-employee relations: failing to solicit and listen to employee input, failing to recognize employees' accomplishments, withholding praise, giving only negative feedback, taking credit for others' accomplishments or ideas, blaming others for one's own mistakes, betraying trusts or confidences, managing up rather than down, micromanaging, withholding critical information, showing distrust, showing favoritism, setting unrealistic goals or deadlines, and failing to help good performers to grow in their careers in the hope of "holding onto them."

Satisfied employees report that their managers are good role models and demonstrate "inspiring leadership." They communicate well and often, they are trustworthy and supportive, they help to create a sense of purpose in the work, and they encourage employee growth and career development.

"Good" Bosses Pay Attention to and Communicate with Their Employees

- They help to make the right job fit in terms of an employee's skills and personal interests.

- They ask their employees about their work and solicit ideas for improvement.

- They ask about their employees' developmental goals and career aspirations.

- They take the time to listen and respond in a way that shows that they care.

- They don't respond in a way that will stop the dialogue ("get real" or "it will never work here").

- They provide frequent, honest feedback to employees about their performance and what is needed for improvement and career growth.

- They recognize and reward good performance and particular accomplishments.

- They learn about their employees by asking employees what motivates them, what they like most about the job, and what problems they have in the job. They ask employees what they like or don't like about "working here" and what might lure them away.

"Good" Bosses Are Trustworthy and Supportive

- They are concerned about their employees' family concerns and work-life balance.

- They are concerned with and promote the physical and mental health of their employees.

- They strive to reduce overload and stress on the job, as much as possible.

- They give credit to others for ideas and contributions to the success of the work.

- They demonstrate flexibility in terms of work hours, attire, and so on.

- They demonstrate respect for employees and honor individual differences, interests, and values.

- They admit their errors and apologize when appropriate.

- They follow up on conversations, suggestions, problems, and so forth.

- They serve as "champions" for their work groups.

- They help to make the work fun and encourage the appropriate use of humor on the job.

"Good" Bosses Help to Create a Sense of Purpose in the Work and Encourage Employee Growth and Career Development

- They know that work that is boring or too stressful is not satisfying.

- They share information about the work and the organization.

- They help employees to develop a sense of pride in the organization and its services or products and help them to see the "big picture."

- They demonstrate their trust in employees' abilities by delegating and providing job autonomy and decision-making authority (for example, through creating and training self-directed work teams), especially in relation to scheduling, processes, and budgeting.

- They solicit ideas for improving work processes and the job.

- They encourage creativity and innovation.

- They try to keep the work interesting. This may include job rotation to provide new challenges and increase understanding of the "big picture." It may include combining related tasks so that jobs are not repetitive and boring and some achievement is perceived.

- They provide coaching and mentoring.

- They question things within the organization that hinder job accomplishment and employee satisfaction.

- They encourage employees to keep up with technologies, processes, and developments in the field in order to improve the work and the employees' skills.

- They help employees to set realistic career goals and to create developmental plans that will further those goals. They check on these at least once each year.

- They help employees to identify and take advantage of developmental opportunities.

- They help employees to network and to make useful connections inside and outside the organization (with internal and external customers, suppliers, trade and professional associations).

- They identify opportunities for development other than simple vertical moves (job enrichment, realignment, relocation, lateral moves).

THE COSTS OF LOSING GOOD EMPLOYEES

Some managers may think that they don't have time to do all these things. The response is: "Consider the time (and costs) required to recruit, interview, hire, assess, train, and integrate new employees to replace the ones who have left." Hard costs include advertising, search firms, travel, entertainment, interviewing, relocation expenses, and sign-on bonuses. Other costs include time spent on interviewing, selecting, orientation, and training; the work that is put on hold while this is done; and the effects on productivity, morale, and customer satisfaction. Unseen costs include the benefits to the competitor of hiring the lost employee and the possible influence of this employee on other employees (to leave). In addition, new hires tend to demand 15 to 35 percent more in pay than the employees they replace. High-tech workers, professionals, and managers cost twice as much as other employees to replace. When looked at from this perspective, one of a manager's primary job responsibilities should be the retention of high-performing employees.

References

American Management Association. (1997). *Retention management: Strategies, practices, trends.* New York: American Management Association, Saratoga Institute.

Hay Group. (1998, December 1). 1998–1999 employee attitudes study. *HR/OD, 8.*

Herzberg, F., Mausner, B., & Snyderman, B.B. (1966). *The motivation to work* (2nd ed.). New York: John Wiley & Sons.

Kaye, B., & Jordan-Evans, S. (1999). *Love 'em or lose 'em: Getting good people to stay.* San Francisco, CA: Berrett-Koehler.

Maslow, A.H. (1943). A theory of human motivation. *Psychological Review, 50*(4), 370–396.

Maslow, A.H. (1970). *Motivation and personality* (2nd ed.). New York: Harper & Row. [Orig. ed., 1954.]

Beverly Kaye *is president of Career Systems International, a publisher of career-development tools, and president of Beverly Kaye and Associates Inc., a consulting and training firm. These enterprises offer instruments, tools, workshops, training of trainer programs, career-development services, coaching and mentoring seminars, and interventions. Dr. Kaye holds a doctorate from UCLA. She is the author of* Up Is Not the Only Way: A Guide to Developing Workforce Talent *and a co-author of* Designing Career Development Systems. *She also is a frequent contributor to the* Annuals.

Sharon Jordan-Evans *is president of the Jordan Evans Group, a leadership-consulting firm that offers one-on-one coaching, organization-development interventions, 360-degree feedback programs, competency development, and other assessment processes for mid- through senior-level management. Ms. Jordan-Evans formerly was a consulting partner and senior vice president of the Change Management Practice at Drake Beam Morin. Her primary work is in the areas of executive coaching, team building, and succession planning. She has a master's degree in organization development.*

CONTRIBUTORS

Kristin J. Arnold, MBA, CPCM
Quality Process Consultants, Inc.
48 West Queens Way
Hampton, VA 23669
   (757) 728-0191 or (800) 589-4733
   fax: (757) 728-0192
   email: karnold@qpcteam.com
   URL: www.qpcteam.com

Robert Alan Black, Ph.D., CSP
Cre8ng People, Places & Possibilities
P.O. Box 5805
Athens, GA 30604
   (706) 353-3387
   fax: (706) 369-1400
   email: alan@cre8ng.com
   URL: www.cre8ng.com

Robert T. Brill, Ph.D.
1217 Lorain Avenue
Bethlehem, PA 18018
   (610) 861-1561
   fax: (610) 807-3800
   email: mertb01@moravian.edu

Heidi A. Campbell
University of Edinburgh
New College—Mound Place
Edinburgh EH1 2LX
Scotland
   011-44-131-650-8945
   email: Heidi.Campbell@ed.ac.uk

Marlene Caroselli
Director
Center for Professional Development
324 Latona Road, Suite 1600
Rochester, NY 14626
   (716) 227-6512
   fax: (509) 696-5405
   email: mccpd@aol.com

Judith A. Colbert, Ph.D.
210–400 Parkside Drive
Waterloo, Ontario, N2L 6E5
Canada
   (519) 884-5328
   email: jcolbert@sentex.net

Michael B. Dahl
Kaehlersbakken 10
4700 Naesved
DK 4700 Naested
Denmark
   (45) 5573-8810
   email: michaelbdahl@hotmail
    .com
[U.S. contact: Margaret Christo,
World Bank, (202) 473-9024,
email: mchristo@worldbank.org]

Peter R. Garber
Manager, Teamwork Development
PPG Industries, Inc.
One PPG Place
Pittsburgh, PA 15272
   (412) 434-3417

Donna L. Goldstein, Ph.D.
Development Associates International
3389 Sheridan Street #309
Hollywood, FL 33021
  (954) 893-0123
  email: devasscint@aol.com

Stephen G. Haines
Centre for Strategic Management
Systems Thinking Press
1420 Monitor Road
San Diego, CA 92110-1545
  (619) 275-6528
  fax: (619) 275-0324
  email: csmintl@san.rr.com
  URL: www.csmintl.com and
    www.systemsthinkingpress.com

Dianne Hofner Saphiere
Director
Nipporica Associates
2516 W. 90th Street
Leawood, KS 66206
  (913) 901-0243
  email: dianne@nipporica.com

Brad Humphrey
Pinnacle Performance Group
7011 Marindale
Shawnee, KS 66218
  (913) 441-3001
  email: brad@pinnacle-performance
    .com

Bonnie Jameson, M.S.
1024 Underhills Road
Oakland, CA 94610
  (510) 832-2597
  fax: (510) 835-8669
  email: BBLjameson@cs.com

Sharon Jordan-Evans
President
Jordan Evans Group
565 Chiswick Way
Cambria, CA 93428
  (805) 927-1432
  fax: (805) 927-7756
  email: sjordevans@aol.com

H.B. Karp
Personal Growth Systems
4932 Barn Swallow Drive
Chesapeake, VA 23321
  (757) 488-4144
  fax: (757) 488-4144
  email: pgshank@aol.com

Beverly Kaye
Beverly Kaye & Associates, Inc.
3545 Alana Drive
Sherman Oaks, CA 91403
  (818) 995-6454
  fax: (818) 995-0984
  email: beverly.kaye@csibka.com

Sara Keenan
2915 Brook Drive
Falls Church, VA 22042
  (703) 377-0072
  fax: (703) 532-1192
  email: keenan_sara@bah.com

M.K. Key, Ph.D.
Key Associates, LLC
144 Second Avenue, North, Suite 150
Nashville, TN 37201
  (615) 255-0011
  fax: (615) 665-1622
  email: keyassocs@mindspring.com

Krista Kurth, Ph.D.
9428 Garden Court
Potomac, MD 20854
  (301) 765-9551
  email: krista@renewalatwork.com

Doug Leigh, Ph.D.
Pepperdine University
Graduate School of Education
  & Psychology
400 Corporate Pointe
Culver City, CA 90230
  (310) 568-2389
  fax: (310) 568-5755
  email: doug@dougleigh.com

Anne M. McMahon
Department of Management
Youngstown State University
One University Plaza
Youngstown, OH 44555-3071
  (330) 742-2350
  fax: (330) 742-1459
  email: ammcmaho@cc.ysu.edu

Gerald V. Miller, Ph.D.
Gerald V. Miller Associates
218 M Street, SW
Washington, DC 20024-3602
  (202) 554-8334
  fax: (202) 554-8710
  email: gvm@radix.net

Rajnish Kumar Misra, Ph.D.
Symbiosis Center for Management
  & HRD
Atur Center, 1068, Gorhle Gloss Road,
  Model Colony
Pune
Maharashtra 411016
India
  91-020-5652374
  fax: 91-020-5672068
  email: rajinish_misra@yahoo.com

Phalgu Niranjana, M.A., M. Phil.
Indian Institute of Management
Rajendra Nagar
Indore, M.P. 452012
India
  91-732-321050
  fax: 91-731-321050
  email: phalgn@iinida.ac.in

Biswajeet Pattanayak, M.A., Ph.D.,
  D. Litt.
Director
North Eastern Institute of Bank
  Management
Jawahar Nagar
Khanpara
Guwahati 781022
India
  91-361-307194/304287/300243/
    304161
  fax: 91-361-308041
  email: bpattanayak@yahoo.com
  or profbp@rediffmail.com

Sanjyot Pethe, Ph.D.
Nisura Institute of Management
Gandlunagar Sarkhej Highway
Ahonedabad, Giynal
India
  email: sanjyol_pethe@hotmail.com

Marcia Ruben
Ruben Consulting Group
520 Pacheco Street
San Francisco, CA 94116
(415) 564-7135
email:
marcia@rubenconsulting.com
URL: www.rubenconsulting.com

Suzanne Adele Schmidt, Ph.D.
18920 Falling Star Road
Germantown, MD 20874
(301) 601-1990
email: suzanne@renewalatwork.com

Jan M. Schmuckler, Ph.D.
3921 Burckhalter Avenue
Oakland, CA 94605
(510) 562-0626
email: jan@lignumvitae.com

C. Louise Sellaro
Department of Management
Youngstown State University
One University Plaza
Youngstown, OH 44555-3071
(330) 742-3071
fax: (330) 742-1459
email: clsellar@cc.ysu.edu

Bob Shaver
University of Wisconsin-Madison
Fluno Center for Executive Education
601 University Avenue
Madison, WI 53715-1035
(800) 292-8964
email: bshaver@bus.wisc.edu

David J. Shevrin, M.P.A.
New Perspectives Group
7364 Oak Tree Drive
Wilbloomfield, WI 48322
(248) 788-9511
email: dshevrin@wwnet.com

Jeff Stokes
Pinnacle Performance Group
7011 Marindale
Shawnee, KS 66218
(913) 441-3001
email: jeff@pinnacle-performance
.com

Helene C. Sugarman
Dynamic Communication
14465 Long Green Drive
Silver Spring, MD 20906
(301) 460-6100
email: hcsugarman@erols.com

Darlene Van Tiem, Ph.D.
1310 Kensington Road
Grosse Pointe Park, MI 48230
(313) 884-4311
email: dvt@umich.edu

Renée Yuengling
1747 Dressage Drive
Reston, VA 20190
(703) 438-8366

CONTENTS OF THE COMPANION VOLUME, THE 2003 ANNUAL: VOLUME 1, TRAINING

---

*See Experiential Learning Activities Categories, p. 6, for an explanation of the numbering system.

**Topic is "cutting edge."